KU-450-556

Richard Brinsley Sheridan

THE RIVALS

AND

THE SCHOOL FOR SCANDAL

(Both Plays slightly Abridged)

EDITED BY

JOHN PEILE, M.A.

Assistant Master at University College School, Frognal,
Hampstead, N.W.; late Scholar of Christ's College, Cambridge

BLACKIE AND SON LIMITED
50 OLD BAILEY LONDON
GLASGOW AND BOMBAY

THE PLAIN-TEXT PLAYS

Sheridan—The Rivals and The School for Scandal
   (Sligatly abridged).

Goldsmith—The Good-Natured Man.

Goldsmith—She Stoops to Conquer.

BLACKIE & SON LTD., 50 OLD BAILEY, E.C. LONDON

Printed and bound in Great Britain

LIFE OF SHERIDAN

RICHARD BRINSLEY SHERIDAN was born in Dublin in 1751. His father, Thomas Sheridan, was then manager of the Theatre Royal of that town. His mother, a woman of great beauty, early showed her powers as a writer of fiction, her novel, *Sidney Biddulph*, being considered by many quite equal to Miss Burney's *Evelina*. She died in 1766.

In 1758 Thomas Sheridan, having failed in Dublin, came with his family to London, where his undoubted ability as a writer gained him the friendship of Dr. Johnson, Samuel Richardson the novelist, and the statesman Wedderburn. In 1762 young Richard and his elder brother were sent to Harrow, where the future dramatist impressed his headmaster, Dr. Parr, with his ability rather than with his industry. Eight years later the family moved to Bath, at that time the most famous and fashionable of health resorts in England. Eager for fame among the literary dilettanti of the town, Sheridan amused himself with the production of a bombastic farce which he named *Jupiter*, and a worthless translation of the Greek author Aristaenetus. A more serious business, as he was soon to learn, was the attachment which he conceived for Miss Linley, whose beautiful features have been immortalized in the "St. Cecilia" of Sir Joshua Reynolds. Despite the opposition of her friends, the lady favoured his suit, and after a brief, but ardent, courtship settled the matter by eloping with her young lover to Calais, where they were secretly married.

In 1774 the young couple took up their abode in London, where Sheridan determined to try again the success of his pen, and in 1775 his first dramatic work, *The Rivals*, was under Garrick's auspices produced at Drury Lane Theatre.

A production, at once witty and inoffensive, might certainly be considered a new departure on the English stage of the eighteenth century, still degraded by the productions of Wycherley, Congreve, George Etherege, and other dramatists of the Restoration. *The Rivals*, though not the immediate success that its author had confidently predicted, was played for sixteen nights, in those times an unusually long period. Its merits will be subsequently discussed at greater length.

In the same year were produced *St. Patrick's Day*, which, except for its style, is a farce of no great merit, and a comic opera, *The Duenna*, of which Mr. Linley composed the music. This was voted the most successful work of its kind since 1728, when Gay took London by storm with *The Beggar's Opera*.

In 1776 the great ambition of Sheridan's life was gratified: he became manager of Drury Lane Theatre. He very wisely determined to revise little-known plays of the great dramatists, producing Congreve's *Old Bachelor*, a translation of Voltaire's *Semiramis*, and *A Trip to Scarborough*, which he himself had adopted from Vanbrugh's *Relapse*. The following year witnessed the first performance of that masterpiece of comedies of manners, *The School for Scandal*, perhaps the most famous of all Sheridan's plays. Scarcely less familiar than Lady Teazle, Mr. Snake, or Joseph Surface, is the character of the immortal Mr. Puff in *The Critic*, which was produced two years later. In style it bears a suspiciously close resemblance to the Duke of Buckingham's little-known comedy, *The Rehearsal*, and has the distinction of being the last in which Garrick appeared. The great actor died in the same year, and Sheridan's sorrow, though undoubtedly sincere, is ill-expressed in a lengthy monody.

But the success of his ventures, and the recognized position which the young dramatist had now attained both among the leaders of fashion and the literary celebrities of his day, now prompted his fertile brain to further ambitions. Politics had always appealed to him, and in 1780, through the influence of his friend, the famous Duchess of Devonshire, he contested successfully, in the Whig interest, the town of Stafford.

The party which he now joined formed the active, though somewhat disunited, opposition to the Tories, of which Lord North was the Prime Minister. Its leading spirits were Burke and Fox. John Wilkes of recent notoriety, the historian Gibbon, and the younger Pitt, just at the beginning of his great career, were others of its prominent members. The country was then seething with discontent at the sovereign's intolerant policy, through which she was soon to lose her American colonies: wars were threatening in France and India, and Ireland was in a state of constant rebellion. The maiden speech of so notable a person as Richard Sheridan was eagerly awaited and greeted with enthusiasm.

But it was not till four years later that an opportunity offered itself of displaying to their utmost advantage his particular talents as an orator. In 1787, in a scene that the master hand of Macaulay has vividly depicted, Warren Hastings was brought to trial, and Sheridan supported Burke in one of the worst charges of the prosecution. Of his speech, unfortunately, only a bare outline remains, but for five hours the whole house sat spellbound " under the wand of the enchanter ", as Pitt himself has reported. It was indeed the crowning point of his career.

In espousing the cause of the French revolutionists, Sheridan offended many of his Whig friends, on whom a perusal of Burke's reflections on the *Causes of the Present Discontents*, and the recent atrocities in Paris, had produced a marked change of feeling. Even Fox considered the bitterness of his attacks to be unprovoked. Still more disastrous to his reputation was his injudicious support, on the occasion of the King's illness in 1789, of a Regency Bill giving absolute powers to the unpopular Prince of Wales.

On the return of a Whig ministry to power he confidently expected that his former friends would reward his past services with a lucrative sinecure. But advancing years had proved powerless to check the imprudence and extravagance which could be graciously ignored or easily excused in a youth of such promise and brilliance.

In 1809 Drury Lane Theatre, the management of which supplied the principal source of his income, was burnt to the ground, and he was practically ruined. Three years later the final blow fell, for at the General Election of 1812 his old constituency rejected him, and he passed from that House, whose debates his eloquence had so often enlivened, to an existence spent almost continuously in the obscurity of a debtor's prison. Deserted by his Prince and patrons, unvisited save by duns and bailiffs, he died at his lodging in Savile Row four years later at the age of sixty-four.

As if in mocking contrast to the squalor and misery of his later years, the procession which followed his coffin to Westminster Abbey consisted of some of the most eminent persons of the day. And to this day the brilliancy of his wit, his charm and versatility, are gratefully remembered, while the laborious efforts of many a profounder scholar have been forgotten.

THE RIVALS

Though with other times the manners and characters so brilliantly portrayed in *The Rivals* are vastly changed, yet the merits of the play remain undisputed.

Nor does the dramatic construction of the play deserve
the censure to which it has been subjected. The self-inflicted
tortures of Faulkland, and the lengthy effusions with which
(in the original text) he and his lady-love give utterance to
their emotions, may possibly have appealed to the sentimental
taste of the period, though they have the inexcusable draw-
back of stopping the action of the play. But the other
characters are endowed with a vitality that will ever prove
attractive. The stern father, whose vigilance and deter-
mination are so easily hoodwinked, the scapegrace son, with
only his natural wit to save him in the trials of an enforced
devotion, the goodhearted country squire, eager to assume
the easy manner of a gentleman of fashion, and the lady
of his devotion, whose sole diversions are in her social
pleasures and sentimental novels—all these were persons
to be met daily in the Bath of the eighteenth century, and
can be easily imagined to exist to-day.

We may well believe that the author rewrote and polished
his work with a scrupulous care that is wanting in the hurried
composition of *The School for Scandal*. But the play bears
the ineradicable stamp of a youthful production. The respective dignity of baronet, squire, and gentlewoman, the easy
bearing of Captain Absolute and Miss Languish, and the
subserviency of their maids and dependents is, indeed, out-
wardly depicted. But in one respect gentry and servants are
exactly alike. The genius which created them formed one
and all in his own image. Determined to show wit in everything, or regarding, as Molière had done a century before
him, the desire to amuse as the sole aim and object of
comedy, he dazzles us with a brilliant display in which all
contrast of light and shade disappears.

But despite the severity of Macaulay's censure, the service
which Richard Sheridan rendered to English drama remains
unimpaired. He showed, as no writer of his day with the
one exception of Goldsmith had deigned to show, that the
English stage had ceased to be merely the sphere of high-
flown sentiment or licentious vulgarity, but that a well-
written drama can offer pleasure as lasting as the most
brilliant fiction, and, in its more serious view, by a cleverly-
drawn picture of the faults and follies of its age, can often
strike home where appeals of statesmen or social reformers
have proved powerless.

THE SCHOOL FOR SCANDAL

IN 1777, two years later than *The Rivals*, appeared *The School for Scandal*, perhaps the most brilliant of all Sheridan's comedies, and certainly the one which shows his creative powers in the flower of their brilliance and spontaneity. "Finished, thank God," he writes on the last sheet, when, after passing through many phases and improvements, the play was finally delivered to its impatient manager—a sentiment which the prompter Hopkins is said to have echoed with a devout "Amen". So great, however, is the skill of the dramatist, and so delicate the touch with which his various characters are depicted, that *The School for Scandal* triumphantly excludes all signs of the labour expended on its composition; indeed, its inherent freshness is not the least of its attractions.

The scene of the play is in London, and its characters represent one and all the fashionable folk of the period who assembled in its drawing-rooms. How few dramatists could have treated persons of such narrow minds, and often of unattractive tastes and interests, in so sympathetic a manner! But Sheridan, in writing, was moved by an earnest desire of proving the mischievous results effected by scandal, to whose pernicious influence so many of his own troubles might have been traced; while at the same time Lady Teazle's repentance, and the final banishment of all the scandal-mongers, show him possessed of the cheerful sentiment that, even among the frivolous and cynical, kindness and simplicity may in the end prevail.

Sentimental, however, the play undoubtedly remains, and incurred Charles Lamb's criticism of misjoining to the sentimental the artificial comedy. But pure comedy, since to avoid being melodramatic it can only touch on the surface of human life, cannot but be artificial. And if the characters appear sentimental it is not the fault of their author, who in this play has purposely avoided any such scenes of love-making such as occur in *The Rivals* whenever Faulkland and Julia are in possession of the stage. And whether its effects be a strong appeal to the heart or, as its author intended, an irresistible triumph of wit, are questions quite beside the point. The success of *The School for Scandal* lies not in its conception, but in the effect that it produces—that it is not so much a play, sentimental or humorous, but something real, and true to life.

The character of Joseph Surface has been compared to Tartuffe in Molière's play, though he seems rather to resemble Iago. Crafty and insinuating, he has succeeded in gaining among his evil-tongued acquaintances too great an esteem to be, in Sir Oliver's opinion, an honest fellow. He is incited, however, by a genuine desire for admiration, while his passion for Lady Teazle is undoubtedly sincere.

His brother Charles reflects in all his actions the average well-born youth of his day. Boisterous and hearty, good-natured to a fault, squandering his own and others' money lavishly, he is redeemed by a real regard for his unknown uncle, and an earnest endeavour to be worthy of the lady whose affections he is so fortunate as to possess.

Lady Teazle is not the common coquette or *intrigante* so frequently portrayed in comedy. Preferring marriage to an elderly bachelor to the monotony of her country life, she devotes all her energies to becoming an adept even in the worst arts of her fashionable acquaintances, till an accident shows her the pitfalls of such a life and recalls her to the paths of virtue and duty.

Sir Peter is the true type of an old English gentleman, at little pains to conceal his disgust at the insincerity of the fashionable world, and full of admiration and real tenderness for the wife of his choice. If Sir Oliver is less convincing and Rowley's much-tried fidelity, perhaps, overdrawn, yet their schemes to test the respective characters of the two Surfaces make up the main incidents of the comedy, and certainly promote its action.

However great the time and trouble expended on composing it, Sheridan must have been highly gratified by the immediate success of his play. It was performed for seventy-three nights, certainly a record run at that period, and realized the satisfactory sum of £10,000. So absorbing was the interest in the new comedy that all anxieties as to the American War, which was then progressing, were forgotten. Sheridan's reputation as a dramatist was now established, provincial managers (Mr. Harris of Bath among the first) were eager to produce a work so sure to be appreciated, and modern taste has pronounced a verdict no less enthusiastic.

THE RIVALS

DRAMATIS PERSONÆ

SIR ANTHONY ABSOLUTE.
CAPTAIN ABSOLUTE (*alias* BEVER-LEY).
FAULKLAND.
ACRES.
SIR LUCIUS O'TRIGGER.
FAG, *servant to Capt. Absolute.*

DAVID, *Acres' servant.*
THOMAS.
MRS. MALAPROP.
LYDIA LANGUISH.
JULIA.
LUCY, *maid to Lydia.*

ACT I

SCENE I. *A Street in Bath*

COACHMAN *crosses the Stage.   Enter* FAG, *looking after him*

Fag. What!—Thomas—sure 'tis he. What!—Thomas!
Thomas!

Coach. Hey! Odds life! Mr. Fag! Give us your hand,
my old fellow servant.

Fag. Excuse my glove, Thomas! I'm glad to see you,
my lad: why, my prince of charioteers, you look as hearty!
But who'd have thought of seeing you in Bath?

Coach. Sure, Master, Madam Julia, Harry, Mrs. Kate,
and the postilion be all come.

Fag. Indeed!

Coach. Aye! Master thought another fit of the gout was
coming to make him a visit, so he'd a mind to gi't the slip,
and whip! we were all off at an hour's warning.

Fag. Aye, aye! hasty in everything or it would not be Sir Anthony Absolute!

Coach. But tell us, Mr. Fag, how does young Master? Sir Anthony will stare to see the Captain here.

Fag. I do not serve Captain Absolute now.

Coach. Why, sure!

Fag. At present I'm employed by Ensign Beverley.

Coach. I doubt, Mr. Fag, you han't changed for the better.

Fag. I have not changed, Thomas.

Coach. No! Why, didn't you say you had left young Master?

Fag. No—well, honest Thomas, I must puzzle you no further; briefly then—Captain Absolute and Ensign Beverley are one and the same person.

Coach. So, so! What, this is some freak, I warrant! Do tell us, Mr. Fag, the meaning o't—you know I ha' trusted you.

Fag. You'll be secret, Thomas?

Coach. As a coach horse.

Fag. Well then, the cause of all this is—Love. Love, Thomas, who (as you may get read to you) has been a masquerader since the days of Jupiter *.

Coach. Aye, aye; I guessed there was a lady in the case: but pray, why does your master pass only for an Ensign? Now if he had shamm'd General indeed——

Fag. Ah, Thomas, there lies the mystery o' the matter. Hark'ee Thomas, my master is in love with a lady of very singular taste: a lady who likes him better as a half-pay Ensign, than if she knew he was son and heir to Sir Anthony Absolute, a baronet of three thousand a year.

Coach. That is an odd taste indeed!—But has she got the stuff, Mr. Fag? Is she rich, hey?

Fag. Rich! why, I believe she owns half the stocks! She could pay the national debt as easily as I could my washer-woman!

Coach. Bravo! faith, I warrant she has a set of thousands * at the least: but does she draw kindly with the Captain?

Fag. As fond as pigeons.

---

* Throughout the text this mark is used to refer the reader to the notes.

Coach. May one hear her name?

Fag. Miss Lydia Languish. But there is an old tough aunt in the way, though by the way she has never seen my master, for he got acquainted with Miss while on a visit in Gloucestershire. But hold, mark, mark! Thomas.

Coach. Zooks! 'tis the Captain. Is that the lady with him?

Fag. No, no! That is Madam Lucy, my master's mistress's maid. They lodge at that house, but I must after him to tell him the news.   *[Exeunt severally*

SCENE II. *A dressing room in* MRS. MALAPROP'S *lodgings.* LYDIA *sitting on a Sofa*

Enter JULIA

Lyd. My dearest Julia, how delighted am I! [*Embrace.*] How unexpected was this happiness!

Julia. True, Lydia, and our pleasure is the greater; but what has been the matter? You were denied to me at first.

Lyd. Ah, Julia, I have a thousand things to tell you! But first inform me what has conjured you to Bath? Is Sir Anthony here?

Julia. He is,—we are all arrived within this hour, and I suppose he will be here to wait on Mrs. Malaprop as soon as he is dressed.

Lyd. Then before we are interrupted, let me impart to you some of my distress! I know your gentle nature will sympathize with me though your prudence may condemn me! My letters have informed you of my whole connection with Beverley;—but I have lost him, Julia! My aunt has discovered our intercourse by a note she intercepted, and has confined me ever since! Yet, would you believe it? She has fallen absolutely in love with a tall Irish baronet she met one night since we have been here, at Lady Macshuffle's rout.

Julia. You jest, Lydia!

Lyd. No, upon my word. She really carries on a kind of correspondence with him, under a feigned name though, till she chooses to be known to him; but it is a Delia or a Celia, I assure you.

Julia. Then, surely, she is more indulgent to her niece?

Lyd. Quite the contrary. Since she has discovered her own frailty, she is become more suspicious of mine. Then I must inform you of another plague!—That odious Acres is to be in Bath to-day: so that I protest I shall be teased out of all spirits!

Julia. Come, come, Lydia, hope for the best—Sir Anthony shall use his interest with Mrs. Malaprop.

Lyd. But you have not heard the worst. Unfortunately I had quarrelled with my poor Beverley, just before my aunt made the discovery, and I have not seen him since to make it up.

Julia. What was his offence?

Lyd. Nothing at all! But, I don't know how it was, as often as we had been together, we had never had a quarrel, and, somehow, I was afraid he would never give me an opportunity. So, last Thursday, I wrote a letter to myself to inform myself that Beverley was at that time paying his addresses to another woman. I signed it *"Your friend unknown"*, showed it to Beverley, charged him with his falsehood, put myself into a violent passion and vowed I'd never see him more.

Julia. If he is as deserving and sincere as you have represented him to me, he will never give you up so. Yet consider, Lydia, you tell me he is but an ensign, and you have thirty thousand pounds.

Lyd. But you know I lose most of my fortune if I marry without my aunt's consent, till of age: and that is what I have determined to do, ever since I knew the penalty. Nor could I love the man who would wish to wait a day for the alternative.

Julia. Nay, this is caprice!

Lyd. What, does Julia tax me with caprice? I thought her lover Faulkland had inured her to it.

Julia. I do not love even *his* faults.

Lyd. But, *à propos*—you have sent to him, I suppose?

Julia. Not yet, upon my word,—nor has he the least idea of my being in Bath. Sir Anthony's resolution was so sudden, I could not inform him of it.

Lyd. Well, Julia, you are your own mistress (though

under the protection of Sir Anthony), yet have you, for
this long year, been a slave to the caprice, the whim, the
jealousy of this ungrateful Faulkland. Tell me candidly,
Julia, had he never saved your life, do you think you should
have been attached to him as you are? Believe me, the
rude blast that overset your boat was a prosperous gale
of love to him.

Julia. Come, Lydia, you are too inconsiderate.

Lyd. Nay, I do but jest.—What's here?

Enter LUCY *in a hurry*

Lucy. Oh, ma'am, here is Sir Anthony Absolute just come
home with your aunt.

Julia. I must go. Sir Anthony does not know I am here.

Lyd. Well, I'll not detain you, coz. Adieu, my dear Julia,
I'm sure you are in haste to send to Faulkland. There,
through my room, you'll find another staircase.

Julia. Adieu.   [*Embraces Lydia and exit*

Lyd. Here, my dear Lucy, take *The Memoirs of a Lady
of Quality** and *The Sentimental Journey.* Hide them. So,
so, now lay *Mrs. Chapone* in sight, and leave *Fordyce's
Sermons* open on the table.

Lucy. Oh, burn it, ma'am, the hairdresser has torn away
as far as *Proper Pride.*

Lyd. Never mind—open at *Sobriety.* Fling me *Lord
Chesterfield's Letters.* Now for 'em.

Enter MRS. MALAPROP* *and* SIR ANTHONY ABSOLUTE

Mrs. Mal. There, Sir Anthony, there sits the deliber-
ate simpleton who wants to disgrace her family and lavish
herself on a fellow not worth a shilling.

Lyd. Madam, I thought you once——

Mrs. Mal. You thought, Miss! I don't know any business you have to think at all. Thought does not become
a young woman. But the point we would request of you
is, that you will promise to forget this fellow, to illiterate*
him, I say, quite from your memory.

Lyd. Ah, madam! our memories are independent of our
wills. It is not so easy to forget.

Mrs. Mal. But I say it is, Miss: there is nothing on earth so easy as to forget, if a person chooses to set about it; and let me tell you, Lydia, these violent memories don't become a young woman.

Sir Ant. Why, sure, she won't pretend to remember when she's ordered not!—aye, this comes of her reading!

Lyd. What crime, madam, have I committed to be treated thus?

Mrs. Mal. Now, don't attempt to extirpate* yourself from the matter: you know I have proof of it. But tell me, will you promise to do as you're bid? Will you take a husband of your friend's choosing?

Lyd. Could I belie my thoughts so far as to give that promise, my actions would as certainly belie my words.

Mrs. Mal. Take yourself to your room. You are fit company for nothing but your own ill humours.

Lyd. Willingly, ma'am—I cannot change for the worse.

[*Exit Lydia*

Mrs. Mal. There's a little hussy for you!

Sir Ant. It's little to be wondered at, ma'am. All this is the natural consequence of teaching girls to read. Had I a thousand daughters, by heaven! I'd as soon have them taught the black art* as their alphabet.

Mrs. Mal. Nay, nay, Sir Anthony, you are an absolute misanthropy.

Sir Ant. In my way hither, Mrs. Malaprop, I observed your niece's maid coming forth from a circulating library!

Mrs. Mal. They are vile places indeed!

Sir Ant. Madam, a circulating library in a town is as an evergreen tree of diabolical knowledge! It blossoms through the year! And depend upon it, Mrs. Malaprop, that they who are so fond of handling the leaves, will long for the fruit at last.

Mrs. Mal. Fie, fie, Sir Anthony, you surely speak laconically*.

Sir Ant. Well, well, Mrs. Malaprop, I will dispute the point no further with you. But to the more important point in debate — you say you have no objection to my proposal?

Mrs. Mal. None, I assure you. I am under no positive

engagement with Mr. Acres, and as Lydia is so obstinate against him, perhaps your son may have better success.

Sir Ant. Well, madam, I will write to the boy directly. He knows not a syllable of this yet, though I have for some time had the proposal in my head. He is at present with his regiment.

Mrs. Mal. We have never seen your son, Sir Anthony, but I hope no objection on his side.

Sir Ant. Objection! let him object if he dare! No, no, Mrs. Malaprop. Jack knows that the least demur puts me in a frenzy directly. Well, I must leave you: and let me beg you, Mrs. Malaprop, to enforce this matter roundly to the girl: take my advice—keep a tight hand: if she rejects this proposal, clap her under lock and key: and if you were just to let the servants forget to bring her dinner for three or four days, you can't conceive how she'd come about.   [*Exit Sir Anthony*

Mrs. Mal. Well, at any rate I shall be glad to get her from under my intuition. She has somehow discovered my partiality for Sir Lucius O'Trigger—sure Lucy can't have betrayed me! No, the girl is such a simpleton, I should have made her confess it. Lucy! Lucy! [*Calls.*]

Lucy. [*Entering*] Did you call, ma'am?

Mrs. Mal. Yes, girl. Did you see Sir Lucius while you was out?

Lucy. No, indeed, ma'am, not a glimpse of him.

Mrs. Mal. Well, come to me presently, and I'll give you another letter to Sir Lucius: but mind, Lucy, if ever you betray what you are entrusted with (unless it be other people's secrets to me) you forfeit my malevolence for ever.
     [*Exit Mrs. Malaprop*

Lucy. Ha! ha! ha! Let me see to what account I have turned my *simplicity* lately. [*Looks at a paper.*] For *abetting Miss Lydia Languish in a design of running away with an Ensign!—in money, sundry times, twelve pounds twelve; gowns, five; hats, ruffles, caps, &c. &c., numberless!* *—From the said Ensign, within this last month, six guineas and a half.* About a quarter's pay! —Item *from Mrs. Malaprop for betraying the young people to her*—when I found matters were likely to be discovered—*two guineas and a* *black padusoy**.—Item, from Mr. Acres, for carrying divers letters—which I never delivered—two guineas and a pair of buckles.—Item, from Sir Lucius O'Trigger, three crowns, two gold pocket pieces and a silver snuff box.* Well done, Simplicity ! Yet I was forced to make my Hibernian believe that he was corresponding, not with the aunt, but with the niece : for though not over rich, I found he had too much pride and delicacy to sacrifice the feelings of a gentleman to the necessities of his fortune. [*Exit*

ACT II

SCENE I.   CAPTAIN ABSOLUTE'S *lodgings*

CAPTAIN ABSOLUTE *and* FAG

Fag. Sir, while I was there Sir Anthony came in : I told him you had sent me to inquire after his health and to know if he was at leisure to see you.

Abso. And what did he say on hearing I was at Bath?

Fag. Sir, I never saw an elderly gentleman more astonished. He started back two or three paces, rapped out a dozen interjectural oaths, and asked what had brought you here?

Abso. Is Mr. Faulkland returned?

Fag. He is above, sir, changing his dress.

Abso. Can you tell me whether he has been informed of Sir Anthony's and Miss Melville's arrival?

Fag. I fancy not, sir : he has seen no one since he came in, but his gentleman, who was with him at Bristol.   I think, sir, I hear Mr. Faulkland coming down——

Abso. Go, tell him I am here.

Fag. Yes, sir. [*Exit Fag*

Abso. Now for my whimsical friend,—if he does not know that his mistress is here, I'll tease him a little before I tell him. [*Enter Faulkland.*] Faulkland, you're welcome to Bath again : you are punctual in your return.

Faulk. Yes, I had nothing to detain me, when I had finished the business I went on.   Well, what news since I left you? How stand matters between you and Lydia?

Abso. Faith, much as they were. I have not seen her since our quarrel. However, I expect to be recalled every hour.

Faulk. Why don't you persuade her to go off with you at once?

Abso. What, and lose two-thirds of her fortune? You forget that, my friend.—No, no, I could have brought her to that long ago.

Faulk. Nay then, you trifle too long—if you are sure of her, propose to the aunt *in your own character*, and write to Sir Anthony for his consent.

Abso. Softly, softly: for though I am convinced my little Lydia would elope with me as Ensign Beverley, yet am I by no means certain that she would take me with the impediment of our friends' consent, a regular humdrum wedding, and the reversion of a good fortune on my side: no, no: I must prepare her gradually for the discovery, and make myself necessary to her, before I risk it.—Well, but Faulkland, you'll dine with us to-day at our hotel?

Faulk. Indeed, I cannot: I am not in spirits to be of such a party.

Abso. By heavens! I shall forswear your company. You are the most teasing, captious *, incorrigible lover.—Do love like a man!

Faulk. I own I am unfit for company.

Abso. But, for heaven's sake! what grounds for apprehension can your whimsical brain conjure up at present?

Faulk. What grounds for apprehension, did you say? Heavens! are there not a thousand? I fear for her spirits —her health—her life! My absence may fret her: her anxiety for my return, her fears for me, may oppress her gentle temper.

Abso. So then, Faulkland, if you were convinced that Julia were well and in spirits you would be entirely content?

Faulk. I should be happy beyond measure—I am anxious only for that.

Abso. Then to cure your anxiety at once—Miss Melville is in perfect health and is at this moment in Bath.

Faulk. Nay, Jack—don't trifle with me.

Abso. She is arrived here with my father within this hour.

Faulk. Can you be serious?

Abso. I thought you knew Sir Anthony better than to be surprised at a sudden whim of this kind. Seriously then, it is as I tell you, upon my honour.

Faulk. My dear friend! Hollo, Du Peigne! my hat.—My dear Jack, now nothing on earth can give me a moment's uneasiness.

Re-enter FAG

Fag. Sir, Mr. Acres, just arrived, is below.

Abso. Stay, Faulkland, this Acres lives within a mile of Sir Anthony, and he shall tell you how your mistress has been ever since you left her. Fag, show the gentleman up.   [*Exit Fag*

Faulk. What, is he much acquainted in the family?

Abso. Oh, very intimate: I insist on your not going: besides, his character will divert you.

Faulk. Well, I should like to ask him a few questions.

Abso. He is likewise a rival of mine—that is of my other self's, for he does not think his friend Captain Absolute ever saw the lady in question: and it is ridiculous enough to hear him complain to me of one Beverley, a concealed skulking rival, who——

Faulk. Hush!—He's here.

Enter ACRES

Acres. Ha! my dear friend, noble captain and honest Jack, how do'st thou? Just arrived, faith, as you see.—Sir, your humble servant. Warm work on the roads, Jack. Odds whips and wheels! I've travelled like a comet, with a tail of dust all the way as long as the Mall*.

Abso. Ah, Bob, you are indeed an eccentric planet, but we know your attraction hither. Give me your leave to introduce Mr. Faulkland to you: Mr. Faulkland, Mr. Acres.

Acres. Sir, I am most heartily glad to see you: sir, I solicit your connections*.—Hey, Jack, what, this is Mr Faulkland, who——

Abso. Aye, Bob, Miss Melville's Mr. Faulkland.

Acres. So! She and your father can be but just arrived before me. I suppose you have seen them? Ah! Mr. Faulkland, you are indeed a happy man.

Faulk. I have not seen Miss Melville yet, sir: I hope she enjoyed full health and spirits in Devonshire?

Acres. Never knew her better in my life, sir—never better. Odds blushes and blooms! She has been as healthy as the German Spa*!

Faulk. There, Jack, there. Oh, by my soul! There is an innate levity in woman that nothing can overcome.—What! happy, and I away!

Acres. What's the matter with the gentleman?

Abso. He is only expressing his great satisfaction at hearing that Julia has been so well and happy—that's all—hey Faulkland?

Faulk. Oh! I am rejoiced to hear it—yes, yes. She has a happy disposition!

Acres. That she has, indeed: then she is so accomplished —so sweet a voice—so expert at her harpsichord*.—There was this time month, how she did chirrup at Mrs. Piano's concert!

Faulk. There again, what do you say to this? You see she has been all mirth and song—not a thought of me!

Abso. Pho! man, is not "music *the food of love*"?*

Faulk. Nay, nay, nay. I'm not sorry that she has been happy—no, no I'm glad of that. I would not have had her sad or sick: but she has been dancing too, I doubt not?

Acres. Aye, truly, was she—at our last race ball——

Faulk. [*In a passion*] There, there! I told you so! I told you so! Oh, she thrives in my absence! Dancing! But her whole feelings have been in opposition with mine: I have been anxious, silent, pensive, sedentary, my days have been hours of care, my nights of watchfulness. She has been all health, spirit! laugh! song! dance! A minuet* I could have forgiven—I say I should not have regarded a minuet— but country dances! I must leave you—I own I am somewhat flurried and that looby* has perceived it.   [*Exit*

Abso. Ha, ha, ha! Poor Faulkland, five minutes since "nothing on earth could give him a moment's uneasiness!"

Acres. The gentleman wasn't angry at my praising his mistress, was he?

Abso. A little jealous, I believe, Bob.

Acres. You don't say so? Ha, ha! jealous of me—that's a good joke: but you know I am not my own property, my dear Lydia has forestalled me. She never could abide me in the country because I used to dress so badly.

Abso. Oh, you'll polish, I doubt not.

Acres. Absolutely I propose so—then if I can find out this Ensign Beverley, odds triggers and flints! I'll make him know the difference o't.

Abso. Spoke like a man!

Enter FAG

Fag. Sir, there is a gentleman below desires to see you. Shall I show him into the parlour?

Abso. Aye, you may.

Acres. Well, I must be gone——

Abso. Stay; who is it, Fag?

Fag. Your father, sir.

Abso. You puppy, why didn't you show him up directly?

[*Exit Fag*

Acres. You have business with Sir Anthony. I expect a message from Mrs. Malaprop at my lodgings. I have sent also to my dear friend, Sir Lucius O'Trigger. Adieu, Jack, we must meet at night, when you shall give me a dozen bumpers to little Lydia.

Abso. That I will with all my heart. [*Exit Acres.*] Now for a parental lecture. I hope he has heard nothing of the business that has brought me here. I wish the gout had held him fast in Devonshire, with all my soul!

Enter SIR ANTHONY

Sir, I am delighted to see you here; and looking so well! Your sudden arrival at Bath made me apprehensive for your health.

Sir Ant. Very apprehensive, I dare say, Jack. What, you are recruiting here, hey?

Abso. Yes, sir, I am on duty.

Sir Ant. Well, Jack, I am glad to see you, though I did not expect it, for I was going to write to you on a little matter of business. Jack, I have been considering that I grow old and infirm and shall probably not trouble you long.

Abso. Pardon me, sir, I never saw you look more strong and hearty; and I pray frequently that you may continue so.

Sir Ant. I hope your prayers may be heard, with all my heart. Well then, Jack, I have been considering that I am so strong and hearty, I may continue to plague you a long time. Now, Jack, I am sensible that the income of your commission, and what I have hitherto allowed you, is but a small pittance for a lad of your spirit. You shall be master of a large estate in a few weeks.

Abso. Let my future, sir, speak my gratitude: I cannot express the sense I have of your munificence. Yet, sir, I presume you would not wish me to quit the army?

Sir Ant. Oh, that shall be as your wife chooses.

Abso. My wife, sir!

Sir Ant. Why, what difference does that make? If you have the estate, you must take it with the live stock on it, as it stands.

Abso. If my happiness is to be the price, I must beg leave to decline the proposition. Pray, sir, who is the lady?

Sir Ant. What's that to you, sir? Come, give me your promise to love and to marry her directly.

Abso. Sir, sir, this is not very reasonable, to summon my affections for a lady I know nothing of!

Sir Ant. I am sure, sir, 't is more unreasonable in you to object to a lady you know nothing of.

Abso. Then, sir, I must tell you plainly, that my inclinations are fixed on another—my heart is engaged to an angel.

Sir Ant. Then pray let it send an excuse. It is very sorry, but business prevents its waiting on her.

Abso. But my vows are pledged to her.

Sir Ant. Let her foreclose *, Jack, let her foreclose: they are not worth redeeming: besides, you have the angel's vows in exchange, I suppose: so there can be no loss there.

Abso. What, sir, promise to link myself to some mass of ugliness! to——

Sir Ant. Zounds sirrah! the lady shall be as ugly as I choose: she shall have a hump on each shoulder: she shall be as crooked as the Crescent, her one eye shall roll like the bull's in Cox's Museum*: she shall have a skin like a mummy—she shall be all this, sirrah! yet I will make you ogle her all day, and sit up all night to write sonnets on her beauty.

Abso. This is reason and moderation indeed!

Sir Ant. None of your sneering, puppy! No grinning, jackanapes!

Abso. Indeed, sir, I never was in a worse humour for mirth in my life.

Sir Ant. There, you sneer again! Don't provoke me—but you rely upon the mildness of my temper—you do, you dog! You play upon the meekness of my disposition! Yet take care—the patience of a saint may be overcome at last!—but mark! I give you six hours and a half to consider of this: If you then agree, without any condition, to do everything on earth that I choose, why—I may in time forgive you. If not, I'll disinherit you, I'll unget you! and I'll never call you Jack again.   [*Exit Sir Anthony, still furious*

Abso. [*Alone*] Mild, gentle, considerate father, I kiss your hands. What a tender method of giving his opinion in these matters Sir Anthony has! I dare not trust him with the truth. I wonder what old wealthy hag it is that he wants to bestow on me!   [*Exit*

SCENE II. *The North Parade*

Enter LUCY

Lucy. So—I shall have another rival to add to my mistress's list. Captain Absolute. However, I shall not enter his name till my purse has received notice in form. Poor Acres is dismissed! Well, I have done him a friendly office, in letting him know that Beverley was here before him. —Sir Lucius is generally more punctual, when he expects to hear from his *dear Dalia,* as he calls her: I wonder he's not here! I have a little scruple of conscience from this deceit: though I should not be paid so well if my hero knew that *Delia* was near fifty, and her own mistress.

Enter SIR LUCIUS O'TRIGGER

Sir Luc. Ha! my little ambassadress, have you got nothing for me?

Lucy. Yes, but I have—I've got a letter for you in my pocket.

Sir Luc. Oh, faith! I guessed you weren't come empty-handed. Well, let me see what the dear creature says.

Lucy. There, Sir Lucius.   [*Gives him a letter*

Sir Luc. [*Reading it*] Faith, she must be very deep read to write this way—though she is rather an arbitrary writer too, for here are a great many poor words pressed into the service of this note, that would get their Habeas Corpus * from any court in Christendom. However, meet me in the evening and I'll give you an answer to this.

                 [*Exit, humming a tune*

Enter FAG

Fag. So, so, madam, I humbly beg pardon.

Lucy. Oh, Mr. Fag, you flurry one so.

Fag. [*Severely*] Come, come, Lucy, here's no one by—so a little less simplicity with a grain or two more sincerity, if you please. You play false with us, madam. I saw you give the baronet a letter. My master shall know this, and if he don't call him out, I will.

Lucy. Ha! ha! ha! you gentlemen's gentlemen are so hasty. That letter was from Mrs. Malaprop, simpleton. She is taken with Sir Lucius's address.

Fag. How! what tastes some people have! Why, I suppose I have walked by her windows a hundred times.—But what says our young lady? Any message to my master?

Lucy. Sad news, Mr. Fag! A worse rival than Acres! Sir Anthony Absolute has proposed his son.

Fag. What, Captain Absolute?

Lucy. Even so—I overheard it all.

Fag. Ha! ha! ha! very good, faith. Goodbye Lucy, I must away with this news.   [*Exeunt severally*

ACT III

SCENE I. *The North Parade*

Enter CAPTAIN ABSOLUTE

Abso. 'T is just as Fag told me, indeed. Whimsical enough, faith! My father wants to *force* me to marry the very girl I am plotting to run away with! He must not know of my connection with her yet awhile. He has too summary a method of proceeding in these matters. However, I 'll read my recantation instantly. My conversion is somewhat sudden indeed—but I can assure him it is very *sincere.* So, so, here he comes. He looks plaguy gruff. [*Steps aside*

Enter SIR ANTHONY

Sir Ant. [*Angrily*] No, I 'll die sooner than forgive him. *Die*, did I say? I 'll live these fifty years to plague him. At our last meeting his impudence had almost put me out of temper. An obstinate, passionate, self-willed boy! Who can he take after? This is my return for getting* him before all his brothers and sisters! For putting him, at twelve years old, into a marching regiment*, and allowing him fifty pounds a year, besides his pay, ever since! But I have done with him : he 's anybody's son for me. I never will see him more—never—never—never—never.

Abso. [*Aside*] Now for a penitential face.

Sir Ant. Fellow, get out of my way!

Abso. Sir, you see a penitent before you.

Sir Ant. I see an impudent scoundrel before me.

Abso. A sincere penitent. I am come, sir, to acknowledge my error, and to submit entirely to your will.

Sir Ant. What 's that?

Abso. I have been revolving and reflecting and considering on your past goodness and kindness and condescension to me.

Sir Ant. Well, puppy?

Abso. Why then, sir, the result of my reflections is—a resolution to sacrifice every inclination of my own to your satisfaction.

Sir Ant. Why then, Jack, my dear Jack, I will now inform you who the lady really is. Nothing but your passion and violence, you silly fellow, prevented my telling you at first. Prepare, Jack, for wonder and rapture—prepare. What think you of Miss Lydia Languish?

Abso. Languish? What, the Languishes of Worcestershire?

Sir Ant. Worcestershire! No. Did you never meet Mrs. Malaprop and her niece, Miss Languish, who came into our country just before you were last ordered to your regiment?

Abso. Malaprop! Languish! I don't remember ever to have heard the names before. Yet, stay—I think I do recollect something. *Languish! Languish!* She squints, don't she? A little red-haired girl?

Sir Ant. Squints? A red-haired girl? No!

Abso. And which is to be mine, sir, the niece or the aunt?

Sir Ant. Why, you unfeeling, insensible puppy, I despise you. The *aunt*, indeed! I've a great mind to marry the girl myself.

Abso. I am entirely at your disposal, sir: if you should think of addressing Miss Languish yourself, I suppose you would have me marry the aunt: and if you should change your mind and take the old lady—'t is the same to me—I'll marry the niece.

Sir Ant. Upon my word, Jack, thou'rt either a very great hypocrite, or—but come, I know your indifference upon such a subject must be all a lie—I'm sure it must—come, now—come, confess, Jack. You have been lying, ha'n't you? But come along with me. I'll write a note to Mrs. Malaprop, and you shall visit the lady directly. [*Exeunt together*

SCENE II. MRS. MALAPROP'S *lodgings*

MRS. MALAPROP, *with a letter in her hand, and* CAPTAIN ABSOLUTE

Mrs. Mal. Your being Sir Anthony's son, Captain, would itself be sufficient, but from the ingenuity of your appearance, I am convinced you deserve the character here given of you.

Abso. Permit me to say, madam, that as I never yet have had the pleasure of seeing Miss Languish, my principal inducement in this affair at present is the honour of being allied to Mrs. Malaprop, of whose intellectual accomplishments, elegant manners, and unaffected learning, no tongue is silent.

Mrs. Mal. Sir, you do me infinite honour! I beg, Captain, you'll be seated. [*They sit. Aside*] He is the very pineapple* of politeness. [*Aloud*] You are not ignorant, Captain, that this giddy girl has somehow contrived to fix her affections on a beggarly, strolling, eavesdropping Ensign whom none of us have ever seen, and nobody knows anything of?

Abso. Oh, I have heard the silly affair before. I'm not at all prejudiced against her on *that* account.

Mrs. Mal. You are very good and very considerate, Captain. I am sure I have done everything in my power since I exploded the affair. I thought she had persisted from corresponding with him: but, behold, this very day I have interceded another letter from the fellow: I believe I have it in my pocket.

Abso. [*Aside*] My last note! Oh, the little traitress Lucy.

Mrs. Mal. There, perhaps you may know the writing.
[*Gives him the letter*

Abso. I think I must have seen the hand before—yes, I certainly must have seen this hand before——

Mrs. Mal. Nay, but read it, Captain.

Abso. [*Reads*] "My soul's idol, my adored Lydia!" Very tender indeed!

Mrs. Mal. Tender! aye and profane too, o' my conscience!

Abso. "I am exceedingly alarmed at the intelligence you send me, the more so as my new rival——"

Mrs. Mal. That's you, sir.

Abso. "Has universally the character of being an accomplished gentleman and a man of honour."—Well, that's handsome enough.

Mrs. Mal. Oh, the fellow has some design in writing so.

Abso. That he had, I'll answer for him, ma'am.

Mrs. Mal. But go on, sir—you'll see presently.

Abso. "As for the old weather-beaten she-dragon that guards you."—Who can he mean by that?

Mrs. Mal. Me, sir! *me*—he means *me*! There—what do you think now?—but go on a little further.

Abso. Impudent scoundrel! "I have a scheme to see you shortly with the old harridan's* consent, and even to make her a go-between in our interview." Was ever such assurance!

Mrs. Mal. Did you ever hear anything like it? He'll elude my vigilance, will he? Yes, yes ha! ha! ha! he's very likely to enter these doors! We'll try who can plot best!

Abso. So we will, ma'am, so we will. Ha! ha! ha! a conceited puppy, ha! ha! ha! But, pray, could I not see the lady for a few minutes now? I should like to try her temper a little.

Mrs. Mal. Well, I don't know. I doubt she is not prepared for a visit of this kind. There is a decorum in these matters.

Abso. O Lord! she won't mind *me*—only tell her Beverley——

Mrs. Mal. Sir!

Abso. Oh, I was going to propose that you should tell her, by way of a jest, that it was Beverley who was below—she'd come down fast enough then. Ha! ha! ha!

Mrs. Mal. 'T would be a trick she well deserves, besides you know the fellow tells her he'll get my consent to see her. Ha! ha! Let him, if he can, I say again. Lydia, come down here. [*Calling.*] The little hussy won't hear. Well, I'll go at once and tell her who it is—she shall know that Captain Absolute is come to wait on her. And I'll make her behave as becomes a young woman. For the present, Captain, your servant. Ah! You're not done laughing yet, I see. "Elude my vigilance!" Yes, yes: ha! ha! ha! [*Exit*

Abso. Ha! ha! ha! One would think now that I might throw off all disguise at once, and seize my prize with security: but such is Lydia's caprice, that to undeceive her were probably to lose her! I'll see whether she knows me. [*Walks aside, pretending to study the pictures*

Enter LYDIA

Lyd. What a scene am I now to go through! I have heard of girls persecuted as I am, who have appealed in behalf of their favoured lover to the generosity of his rival: suppose I were to try it—there stands the hated rival—an officer, too. But oh! how unlike my Beverley! I wonder he don't begin—truly he seems a very negligent wooer—quite at his ease, upon my word! I'll speak first—Mr. Absolute.

Abso. [*Turning towards her*] Ma'am!

Lyd. Oh heavens! Beverley!

Abso. Hush! hush! be not surprised!

Lyd. I am astonished and so terrified! and so overjoyed! for Heaven's sake, how came you here?

Abso. Briefly, I have deceived your aunt. I was informed that my new rival was to visit here this evening, and contriving to keep him away, have passed myself on her as Captain Absolute.

Lyd. Oh, charming! And she really takes you for young Absolute?

Abso. Oh, she's convinced of it.

Lyd. Ha! ha! ha! I can't forbear laughing to think how her sagacity is overreached!

Abso. But we trifle with our precious moments—such another opportunity may not occur. Then let me now conjure my kind, my condescending angel to fix the time when I may rescue her from undeserving persecution.

Lyd. Will you then, Beverley, consent to forfeit that portion of my paltry wealth?—that burden on the wings of love? [*Aside*] Now could I fly with him to the Antipodes! But my persecution is not yet come to a crisis.

Re-enter MRS. MALAPROP, *listening*

Mrs. Mal. [*Aside*] I am impatient to know how the little hussy deports herself.

Lyd. Think not the idle threats of my ridiculous aunt can ever have any weight with me.

Mrs. Mal. Very dutiful, upon my word!

Lyd. Let her choice be Captain Absolute, but Beverley is mine.

Mrs. Mal. I am astonished at her assurance! To his face! This to his face!

Abso. Then let me enforce my suit. [*Kneeling.*]

Mrs. Mal. Aye, poor young man! Down on his knees entreating for pity! I can contain no longer. [*Advancing angrily.*] Why, thou vixen! I have overheard you. Captain Absolute, I know not how to apologize for her shocking rudeness.

Lyd. Nay, madam, what do you charge me with now?

Mrs. Mal. Why, thou unblushing rebel, didn't you tell this gentleman to his face that you loved another better? Didn't you say you would never be his?

Lyd. No, madam, I did not.

Mrs. Mal. Good heavens! What assurance! Didn't you boast that Beverley, that stroller Beverley, possessed your heart? Tell me that, I say.

Lyd. 'T is true, ma'am, and none but *Beverley*——

Mrs. Mal. Hold! hold! Assurance! you shall not be so rude.

Abso. Nay, pray Mrs. Malaprop, don't stop the young lady's speech: she's very welcome to talk thus—it does not hurt *me* in the least, I assure you.

Mrs. Mal. You are too good, Captain — too amiably patient—but come with me, miss. Let us see you again soon, Captain, remember what we have fixed.

[*Exeunt. Beverley kisses his hand to Lydia, whom
Mrs. Malaprop stops from speaking*

SCENE III. ACRES' *lodgings*

Acres. [*Practising his dancing*] Sink, slide, coupée*. I can walk a minuet easy enough when I am forced, and I have been accounted a good stick in a country dance. But these outlandish heathen allemandes and cotillons* are quite beyond me!

Enter Servant

Servant. Here is Sir Lucius O'Trigger to wait on you, sir.

Acres. Show him in.

Enter Sir Lucius

Sir Luc. Mr. Acres, I'm delighted to embrace you.

Acres. My dear Sir Lucius, I kiss your hands.

Sir Luc. Pray, my friend, what has brought you so suddenly to Bath?

Acres. Faith! I have followed Cupid's Jack-a-lantern *, and find myself in a quagmire at last. In short, I have been very ill used, Sir Lucius. I don't choose to mention names, but look on me as on a very ill-used gentleman.

Sir Luc. Pray, what is the cause. I ask no names.

Acres. Mark me, Sir Lucius, I fall as deep as need be in love with a young lady—her friends take my part—I follow her to Bath—send word of my arrival: and receive answer that the lady is to be otherwise disposed of. This, Sir Lucius, I call being ill used.

Sir Luc. Very ill, upon my conscience. Pray, can you divine the cause of it?

Acres. Why, there's the matter: she has another lover, one Beverley, who, I am told, is now in Bath. Odds slanders and lies! He must be at the bottom of it.

Sir Luc. A rival in the case, is there? And you think he has supplanted you unfairly.

Acres. Unfairly! to be sure he has. He never could have done it fairly.

Sir Luc. Then sure you know what is to be done!

Acres. Not I, upon my soul!

Sir Luc. We wear no swords here, but you understand me?

Acres. What! fight him!

Sir Luc. Aye, to be sure, what can I mean else?

Acres. Odds balls and barrels! Say no more,—I'm braced for it. The thunder of your words has soured the milk of human kindness in my breast! As the man in the play says, "I could do such deeds——"

Sir Luc. Come, come, there must be no passion at all in the case—these things should always be done civilly.

Acres. I *must* be in a passion, Sir Lucius, I *must* be in a rage. Dear Sir Lucius, let me be in a rage, if you love me. Come, here's pen and paper. [*Sits down to write.*] I would the ink were red. Indite, I say, indite! How shall I begin?

Sir Luc. Pho! pho! do the thing decently, and like a Christian. Begin now—"Sir,——"

Acres. That's too civil by half.

Sir Luc. "To prevent the confusion that might arise——"

Acres. Well——

Sir Luc. "From our both addressing the same lady——"

Acres. Aye, there's the reason—"same lady"—well?

Sir Luc. "I shall expect the honour of your company——"

Acres. But I'm not asking him to dinner.

Sir Luc. Pray, be easy.

Acres. Well, then, "the honour of your company——"

Sir Luc. "To settle our pretensions——"

Acres. Well?

Sir Luc. Let me see,—aye. King's Mead Fields* will do—"in King's Mead Fields."

Acres. So that's done. Well, I'll fold it up presently: my own crest—a hand and a dagger shall be the seal.

Sir Luc. You see now this little explanation will put a stop at once to all confusion or misunderstanding that might arise between you.

Acres. Aye, we fight to prevent any misunderstanding.

Sir Luc. Now, I'll leave you to fix your own time. Take my advice and you'll decide it this evening if you can: then let the worst come of it, 't will be off your mind to-morrow.

Acres. [*Gloomily*] Very true.   [*Exit Sir Lucius*

ACT IV

SCENE I. ACRES' *lodgings*

ACRES *and* DAVID

Acres. But, David, now, you don't think there is such very, very, *very* great danger, hey?   People often fight without any mischief done.

Dav. By the mass, I think 't is ten to one against you. Oons! here to meet some lionhearted fellow, I warrant you, with his double-barrelled swords and cut-and-thrust pistols.

Acres. Zounds! I *won't* be afraid. Odds fire and fury, you shan't make me afraid. Here is the challenge and I have sent for my dear friend Jack Absolute to carry it. Out, you poltroon! You haven't the valour of a grasshopper.

Enter Servant

Servant. Captain Absolute, sir.

Acres. Oh, show him up.   [*Exit Servant*

Dav. Well, Heaven send we may be all alive this time to-morrow!

Acres. What's that?   Don't provoke me, David!

Dav. [*Whimpering*] Goodbye, master.

Acres. Get along, you cowardly, dastardly, croaking raven.
                                                   [*Exit David*

Enter CAPTAIN ABSOLUTE

Abso. What's the matter, Bob?

Acres. A vile, sheep-hearted blockhead! If I hadn't the valour of St. George and the Dragon to boot *——

Abso. But what did you want with me, Bob?

Acres. [*Producing letter*] Oh! There——

Abso. [*Reading*] "To Ensign Beverley."   So. [*Aside*] What's going on now! Well, what's this?

Acres. A challenge!

Abso. But what have I to do with this?

Acres. Why, as I think you know something of this fellow, I want you to find him out for me and give him this mortal defiance.

Abso. Well, give it to me, and trust me he gets it.

Acres. You are very kind. What it is to have a friend! You couldn't be my second, could you, Jack?

Abso. Why, no, Bob—not in this affair,—it would not be quite so proper.

Acres. Well, then, I must get my friend Sir Lucius I shall have your good wishes, however, Jack?

Abso. Whenever he meets you, believe me.

Enter Servant

Servant. Sir Anthony Absolute is below, inquiring for the Captain.

Abso. [*Rising*] I'll come instantly. Well, my little hero, success attend you.

Acres. Stay,—stay, Jack. If Beverley should ask you what kind of a man your friend Acres is, do tell him I am a devil of a fellow—will you, Jack?

Abso. To be sure, I shall. I'll say you are a determined dog, hey, Bob?

Acres. Aye, do, do,—and if that frightens him, perhaps he mayn't come. So tell him I generally kill a man a week; will you, Jack?

Abso. [*Going*] I will, I will.

Acres. Remember, Jack, a determined dog!

Abso. Aye, aye, "Fighting Bob!"   [*Exit*

SCENE II. MRS. MALAPROP'S *lodgings*

Mrs. Mal. Why, thou perverse one! Tell me what you can object to him? Isn't he a handsome man? tell me that. A genteel man? a pretty figure of a man?

Lydia. [*Aside*] She little thinks whom she is praising. [*Aloud*] So is Beverley, ma'am.

Mrs. Mal. No caparisons, miss, if you please. Caparisons don't become a young woman. No. Captain Absolute is indeed a fine gentleman!

Lydia. [*Aside*] Aye, the Captain Absolute *you* have seen.

Mrs. Mal. Then he's *so* well bred; so full of alacrity and adulation*! and has *so much* to say for himself; in such good language too. Then his presence is so noble. I protest, when I saw him, I thought of what Hamlet says in the play*;

> "Hesperian curls—the front of Job himself!—
> An eye, like March, to threaten at command!—
> A station, like Harry Mercury, new"—

something about kissing on a hill, however the similitude struck me directly.

Lydia. [*Aside*] How enraged she'll be presently, when she discovers her mistake!

Enter Servant

Servant. Sir Anthony and Captain Absolute are below, ma'am.

Mrs. Mal. Show them up here. [*Exit Servant.*] Now, Lydia, I insist on your behaving as becomes a young woman. Show your good breeding at least, though you have forgot your duty.

Lydia. Madam, I have told you my resolution. I shall not only give him no encouragement, but I won't even speak to, or look at him.

[*Sits down, back to the door, her face hidden*

Enter SIR ANTHONY and CAPTAIN ABSOLUTE

Sir Ant. Here we are, Mrs. Malaprop, come to mitigate the frowns of unrelenting beauty, and difficulty enough I had to bring this fellow. I don't know what is the matter; but if I had not held him by force, he'd have given me the slip.

Mrs. Mal. You have infinite trouble, Sir Anthony, in the affair. I am ashamed for the cause! Lydia, Lydia [*Aside to her*], rise, I beseech you! Pay your respects.

Abso. [*Aside*] What shall I do? [*To his father*] You see, sir, she won't even look at me, whilst you are here. I knew she wouldn't. I told you so. Let me entreat you, sir, to leave us together. [*Continues to expostulate with his father*

Lydia. [*Aside*] I wonder I ha'n't heard my aunt exclaim

yet! sure, she can't have looked at him. Perhaps their regimentals are alike, and she is something blind.

[*Absolute makes signs to Mrs. Malaprop to leave them together*

Mrs. Mal. Sir Anthony, shall we leave them together? [*Shaking Lydia*] Oh, you stubborn little vixen!

Sir Ant. Not yet, ma'am, not yet. [*To his son*] What are you at? Unlock your jaws, sirrah, or——

Abso. [*Aside*] Now, Heaven send she may be too sullen to look round! I must disguise my voice. [*Approaching Lydia, but speaking in a low hoarse tone*] Will not Miss Languish lend an ear to the mild accents of true love? Will not——

Sir Ant. [*Angrily*] What ails the fellow? Why don't you speak out? not stand croaking like a frog in a quinsy!

Abso. The—the—excess of my awe and my—my—my modesty quite choke me.

Sir Ant. Ah, your modesty again. I tell you what, Jack; if you don't speak out directly and glibly too, I shall be in such a rage! Mrs. Malaprop, I wish the lady would favour us with something more than a side-front.

[*Mrs. Malaprop seems to chide Lydia*

Abso. [*Aside*] So all will out, I see. [*Advances towards Lydia and speaks softly*] Be not surprised, my Lydia, suppress all surprise at present.

Lydia. [*Aside*] Heavens, 't is Beverley's voice! Sure he can't have imposed upon Sir Anthony too. [*Looks round gradually and then starts up.*] Is this possible? my Beverley! how can this be? My Beverley!

Abso. [*Aside*] Ah, 't is all over.

Sir Ant. Beverley, Beverley! What can the girl mean? This is my son, Jack Absolute.

Mrs. Mal. For shame, hussy, for shame! Your head runs so on that fellow, that you have him always in your eyes. Beg Captain Absolute's pardon directly.

Lydia. I see no Captain Absolute, but my loved Beverley.

Sir Ant. The girl's mad! her brain's turned by reading! Oh, she's mad as Bedlam!—or has this fellow been playing us a rogue's trick? Come here, sirrah, who are you?

Abso. Faith, sir, I am not quite clear myself; but I 'll endeavour to recollect.

Sir Ant. Are you my son or not?

Mrs. Mal. Aye, sir, who are you? O mercy! I begin to suspect.

Abso. [*Aside*] Ye powers of impudence, befriend me! Sir Anthony, that I sincerely believe myself to be your son, I hope my duty has always shown. Mrs. Malaprop, I am your most respectful admirer, and shall be proud to add affectionate nephew. I need not tell my Lydia that she sees her faithful Beverley, who, knowing the singular generosity of her temper, assumed that name and station, which has proved a test of the most disinterested love, which he now hopes to enjoy in a more elevated character.

Lydia. [*Sullenly*] So, there is to be no elopement after all!

Sir Ant. Upon my soul, Jack, thou art a very impudent fellow! To do you justice, I think I never saw a piece of more consummate assurance! I wonder you an't ashamed to hold up your head.

Abso. 'T is with difficulty, sir. I *am* confused, very much confused, as you must perceive.

Mrs. Mal. O, Lud, Sir Anthony! A new light beats in upon me! Hey, how! what! Captain, did *you* write the letter then? What—am I to thank *you* for the elegant compilation of " an old weather-beaten she-dragon ", hey?

Abso. Dear sir! My modesty will be overpowered at last, if you don't assist me. I shall certainly not be able to stand it!

Sir Ant. Come, come, Mrs. Malaprop, we must forget and forgive. Odds life! matters have taken so clever a turn all of a sudden that I could find in my heart to be so good-humoured! and so gallant! Hey! Mrs. Malaprop!

Mrs. Mal. Well, Sir Anthony, since you desire it, we will not anticipate the past.

Sir Ant. Come, we must leave them together: Mrs. Malaprop, they long to fly into each other's arms, I warrant. We 'll not disturb their tenderness—theirs is the time of life for happiness! [*Singing*] " Youth's a season made for joy "

—hey? Odds life! I'm in such spirits,—I don't know what I could not do. Permit me, ma'am.

> [*Exit, singing and handing Mrs. Malaprop.*
> *Lydia sits sullenly in her chair*

Abso. [*Aside*] So much thought bodes me no good. [*Aloud*] So grave, Lydia!

Lydia. Sir!

Abso. [*Aside*] So! I thought as much. That monosyllable has froze me! [*Aloud*] What, Lydia, now that we are as happy in our friends' consent as in our mutual vows ——

Lydia. [*Angrily*] *Friends' consent*, indeed!

Abso. Come, come, we must lay aside some of our romance —a little wealth and comfort may be endured after all. And for your fortune, the lawyers shall make such settlements as——

Lydia. Lawyers! I hate lawyers!

Abso. Nay then, we'll not wait for their lingering forms, but instantly procure the licence, and——

Lydia. The licence! I hate licence!

Abso. Oh, my love! be not so unkind! thus let me entreat—— [*Kneeling.*]

Lydia. Pshaw!—what signifies kneeling, when you know I *must* have you?

Abso. [*Rising*] Nay, madam, there shall be no constraint put upon your inclinations, I promise you. If I have lost your heart—I will resign the rest. [*Aside*] I must try what a little spirit will do.

Lydia. [*Softening*] 'T is your own doing, sir,—I—I—suppose you are perfectly satisfied?

Abso. Oh, most certainly—sure, now, this is much better than being in love! Ha! ha! ha! there's some spirit in *this*! What signifies breaking some scores of solemn promises: all that's of no consequence, you know.

> [*Exit angrily*

Lydia. [*Bursting into tears*] There's no bearing his insolence.

SCENE III. *The North Parade*

Enter CAPTAIN ABSOLUTE

Abso. To what fine purpose I have been plotting! A noble reward for all my schemes, upon my soul! A little gipsy—I did not think her romance could have made her so absurd either. I never was in a worse humour in my life! I could cut my own throat, or any other person's, with the greatest pleasure in the world!

Enter SIR LUCIUS *from behind*

Sir Luc. [*Aside*] Oh, faith! I'm in the luck of it. I never could have found him in a sweeter temper for my purpose—to be sure I'm just come in the nick! Now to enter into conversation with him, and so quarrel genteelly. [*Advancing towards Absolute*] With regard to that matter, Captain, I must beg leave to differ in opinion with you.

Abso. Upon my word, then, you must be a very subtle disputant: because, sir, I happened just then to be giving no opinion at all.

Sir Luc. That's no reason. For give me leave to tell you, a man may *think* an untruth as well as speak one.

Abso. Very true, sir, but if a man never utters his thoughts, I should think they might stand a chance of escaping controversy.

Sir Luc. Then, sir, you differ in opinion with me, which amounts to the same thing.

Abso. Hark'ee, Sir Lucius,—if I had not before known you to be a gentleman, upon my soul I should not have discovered it at this interview: for what you can drive at unless you mean to quarrel with me, I cannot conceive.

Sir Luc. I humbly thank you, sir, for the quickness of your apprehension*. [*Bowing*] You have named the very thing I would be at.

Abso. Very well, sir, I shall certainly not balk your inclinations: but I should be glad if you would please explain your motives.

Sir Luc. Pray, sir, be easy—the quarrel is a very pretty

quarrel as it stands—we should only spoil it by trying to explain it. However, if it's the same to you, Captain, I should take it as a particular kindness if you'd let us meet in King's Mead Fields, as a little business will call me there about six o'clock, and I may dispatch both matters at once.

Abso. 'T is the same to me exactly. A little after six, then, we will discuss this matter more seriously.

Sir Luc. If you please, sir : there will be very pretty small sword light, though it won't do for a long shot. So that matter's settled! and my mind's at ease. [*Exit Sir Lucius*

Enter FAULKLAND, *meeting* CAPTAIN ABSOLUTE

Abso. Well met, I was going to look for you. A good-natured Irishman here has [*Mimicking Sir Lucius*] begged leave to have the pleasure of cutting my throat, and I mean to indulge him—that's all.

Faulk. Prithee, be serious.

Abso. 'T is fact, upon my soul. Sir Lucius O'Trigger—you know him by sight—for some affront, which I am sure I never intended, has obliged me to meet him this evening at six o'clock : 't is on that account I wished to see you —you must go with me.

Faulk. Nay, there must be some mistake, sure. Sir Lucius shall explain himself—and I dare say matters may be accommodated : but this evening did you say?—I wish it had been any other time.

Abso. Why? There will be light enough : there will (as *Sir Lucius* says) "be very pretty small sword light, though it will not do for a long shot".

Faulk. But I am myself a good deal ruffled by a difference I have had with Julia—my vile tormenting temper has made me treat her so cruelly, that I shall not be myself till we are reconciled.

Abso. By heavens! Faulkland, you don't deserve her.
[*Exit*

Faulk. I feel his reproaches; yet I would not change this too exquisite nicety* for the gross content with which he tramples on the thorns of love. His engaging me in this duel has started an idea in my head which I will instantly pursue. I'll use it as the touchstone of Julia's sincerity and disinterestedness. *[Exit Faulkland*

ACT V

SCENE I. JULIA's *dressing-room.* JULIA *alone at her work*

Enter LYDIA

Lyd. O Julia, I am come to you with such an appetite for consolation. Lud, child, whatever vexations you may have, I can assure you, mine surpasses them. You know who Beverley proves to be?—But I don't care. I'll never have him.

Julia. Nay, Lydia.

Lyd. Why, is it not provoking? When I thought we were coming to the prettiest distress imaginable, to find myself made a mere Smithfield* bargain of at last. There had I projected one of the most sentimental elopements! so becoming a disguise, so amiable a ladder of ropes. Conscious moon,—four horses,—Scotch parson*,—with much surprise to Mrs. Malaprop,—and such paragraphs in the newspapers. Oh, I shall die with disappointment!

Julia. I don't wonder at it!

Lyd. Now,—sad reverse—what have I to expect but, after a deal of flimsy preparation, with a bishop's licence, and my aunt's blessing, to go simpering up to the altar: or perhaps be cried three times* in a country church and have an unmannerly fat clerk ask the consent of every butcher in the parish to join John Absolute and Lydia Languish, spinster! Oh! that I should live to hear myself called spinster!

Julia. If I were in spirits, Lydia, I should chide you only by laughing at you: but it suits more the situation of my mind, at present, earnestly to entreat you not to let a man who loves you with sincerity suffer that unhappiness from your caprice, which I know too well caprice can inflict.

Lyd. O Lud! What has brought my aunt here?

Enter MRS. MALAPROP, FAG, *and* DAVID

Mrs. Mal. So! so! Here's fine work—here's a fine suicide going on in the fields! and Sir Anthony not to be found to prevent the antistrophe!*

Julia. For heaven's sake, madam, what's the meaning of this?

Mrs. Mal. That gentleman can tell you—'t was he enveloped* the affair to me.

Lyd. [*To Fag*] Do, sir, will you, inform us?

Fag. Ma'am, I should hold myself very deficient in every requisite that forms the man of breeding, if I delayed a moment to give all the information in my power to a lady so deeply interested in the affair as you are.

Lyd. But quick! quick, sir! Who are engaged in this?

Fag. Faith, ma'am, one is a young gentleman whom I should be very sorry anything was to happen to—a very pretty-behaved gentleman! We have lived much together, and always on terms——

Lyd. But who is this? Who! Who! Who!

Fag. My master, ma'am,—my master—I speak of my master.

Lyd. Heavens! What, Captain Absolute!

Mrs. Mal. Oh, to be sure, you are frightened now!

Julia. But who are with him, sir?

Fag. As to the rest, ma'am, this gentleman can inform you better than I.

Julia. [*To David*] Do speak, friend.

David. Look'ee, ma'am—by the mass! there's mischief going on.

Julia. But who is there beside Captain Absolute, friend?

David. My poor master—under favour for mentioning him first. You know me, my lady—I am David—and my master, of course is, or *was*, Squire Acres. Then come Squire Faulkland and Sir Lucius O'Trigger.

Mrs. Mal. Sir Lucius O'Trigger! Oh, mercy! Have they drawn poor little dear Sir Lucius into the scrape? Why, how you stand, girl! You have no more feeling than one of the Derbyshire petrifactions*!

Lyd. What are we to do, madam?

Mrs. Mal. Why, fly with the utmost felicity*, to be sure, to prevent mischief!—Here, friend [*To David*], you can show us the place.

Fag. [*With dignity*] If you please, ma'am, I will conduct you.—David, do you look for Sir Anthony. [*Exeunt, he talking*

SCENE II. *South Parade*

Enter CAPTAIN ABSOLUTE, *putting his sword under his greatcoat.*

Abso. A sword seen in the streets of Bath would raise as great an alarm as a mad dog. How provoking this is in Faulkland! Never punctual! I shall be obliged to go without him at last. Ah, here's Sir Anthony! How shall I escape him?   [*Muffles up his face and takes a circle to go off*

Enter SIR ANTHONY

Sir Ant. How one may be deceived at a little distance! Only that I see he don't know me, I could have sworn that was Jack! Hey!—it is. Why, Jack—what are you afraid of? hey!—sure I'm right. Why, Jack,—Jack Absolute!
[*Goes up to him*

Abso. Really, sir, you have the advantage of me: I don't remember ever to have had the honour—my name is Saunderson, at your service.   [*Exit, hastily*

Sir Ant. Sir, I beg your pardon—I took you——

Enter DAVID, *running*

Dav. Stop him! stop him! Murder! thief! fire! Stop, fire! stop, fire!—Oh, Sir Anthony—call! call! bid 'un stop! Murder! fire!

Sir Ant. Fire! Murder! Where?

Dav. Aye, please you, Sir Anthony, there's all kinds of murder, all sorts of slaughter to be seen in the fields: there's fighting going on, sir—bloody sword and gun fighting!

Sir Ant. Who are going to fight, dunce*?

Dav. Everybody that I know of, Sir Anthony: everybody is going to fight, my poor master, Sir Lucius O'Trigger, your son, the captain——

Sir Ant. Oh, the dog! I see his tricks: do you know the place?

Dav. King's Mead Fields.

Sir Ant. You know the way?

Dav. Not an inch: but I'll call the mayor—aldermen—constables—churchwardens—and beadles—we can't be too many to part them.

Sir Ant. Come along! Give me your shoulder! we'll get assistance as we go—the lying villain! Well, I shall be in a frenzy. So, this was his story! I'll Saunderson him!

[*Exeunt*

SCENE III. *King's Mead Fields*

SIR LUCIUS *and* ACRES *with pistols*

Acres. By my valour! then, Sir Lucius, forty yards is a good distance. Odds levels and aims!—I say it is a good distance.

Sir Luc. Is it for muskets or for small field-pieces? Upon my conscience, Mr. Acres, you must leave these things to me. Stay now, I'll show you. [*Measures paces along the stage.*] There, now, that is a very pretty distance, a pretty gentleman's distance.

Acres. [*Gloomily*] Why, we might as well fight in a sentry box! I tell you, Sir Lucius, the farther he is off, the cooler I shall take my aim.

Sir Luc. Faith! then I suppose you would aim at him best of all if he was out of sight!

Acres. No, Sir Lucius, but I should think forty or eight and thirty yards——

Sir Luc. Pho! pho! nonsense! three or four feet between the mouths of your pistols is as good as a mile. But tell me now, Mr. Acres, in case of an accident, is there any little will or commission I could execute for you?

Acres. I am much obliged to you, Sir Lucius—but I don't understand——

Sir Luc. Why, you may think there's no being shot at without a little risk,—and if an unlucky bullet should carry a quietus with it—I say it will be no time then to be bothering you about family matters.

Acres. A quietus!

Sir Luc. For instance, now—if that should be the case—would you choose to be pickled and sent home?—or would it be the same to you to lie here in the Abbey*? I'm told there is very snug lying in the Abbey.

Acres. Pickled! snug lying in the Abbey! Odds tremors! Sir Lucius, don't talk so! If I wa'n't with you, I should almost think I was afraid—if my valour should leave me! Valour will come and go.

Sir Luc. Then pray keep it fast while you have it.

Acres. Sir Lucius—I doubt it is going—yes—my valour is certainly going!—it is sneaking off! I feel it oozing out as it were at the palms of my hands!

Sir Luc. Your honour—your honour. Here they are.

Acres. Oh, mercy! now—that I was safe at Clod Hall! or could be shot before I was aware!

Enter FAULKLAND *and* ABSOLUTE

Sir Luc. Gentlemen, your most obedient.—Hah! what, Captain Absolute! So, I suppose sir, you are come here, just like myself—to do a kind office, first for your friend—then to proceed to business on your own account.

Acres. What, Jack!—my dear Jack!—my dear friend!

Abso. Hark 'ee, Bob, Beverley's at hand.

Sir Luc. Well, Mr. Acres—I don't blame your saluting the gentleman civilly. So, Mr. Beverley [*To Faulkland*], if you'll choose your weapons, the captain and I will measure the ground.

Faulk. My weapons, sir?

Acres. Odds life! Sir Lucius, I'm not going to fight Mr. Faulkland: these are my particular friends.

Sir Luc. What, sir, did you not come here to fight Mr. Acres?

Faulk. Not I, upon my word, sir.

Sir Luc. Well, now, that's most provoking! But I hope, Mr. Faulkland, as there are three of us come on purpose for the game, you won't be so cantankerous as to spoil the party by sitting out.

Abso. Oh, pray, Faulkland, fight to oblige Sir Lucius.

Faulk. Nay, if Mr. Acres is so bent on the matter——

Acres. No, no, Mr. Faulkland—I'll bear my disappointment like a Christian. Look 'ee, Sir Lucius, there's no occasion at all for me to fight: and if it is the same to you, I'd as lieve let it alone.

Sir Luc. Observe me, Mr. Acres.—I must not be trifled with. You have certainly challenged somebody, and you came here to fight him. Now, if that gentleman is willing to represent him—I can't see, for my soul, why it isn't just the same thing.

Acres. Why, no—Sir Lucius—I tell you 't is one Beverley I've challenged—a fellow, you see, that dare not show his face! If *he* was here, I'd make him give up his pretensions directly!

Abso. Hold, Bob—let me set you right—there is no such man as Beverley in the case. The person who assumed the name is before you: and as his pretensions are the same in both characters, he is ready to support them in whatever way you please.

Sir Luc. Well, this is lucky, Now you have an opportunity——

Acres. What, quarrel with my dear friend Jack Absolute —not if he were fifty Beverleys! Sir Lucius, you would not have me so unnatural.

Sir Luc. Upon my conscience, Mr. Acres, your valour has *oozed* away with a vengeance!

Acres. Not in the least! Odds backs and abettors! I'll be your second with all my heart—and if you should get a *quietus*, you may command me entirely. I'll get you *snug lying* in the *Abbey here*: or *pickle* you, and send you over to Blunderbuss Hall, or anything of the kind, with the greatest pleasure.

Sir Luc. Pho! pho! you are little better than a coward.

Acres. Mind, gentlemen, he calls me *coward*; coward was the word, by my valour!

Abso. Nay, Sir Lucius, you can't have a better second than my friend Acres. He is a most *determined dog*— called in the country *Fighting Bob*. He generally *kills a man a week*: don't you, Bob?

Acres. Aye—at home!

Sir Luc. Well, then, Captain, 't is we must begin — so come out, my little counsellor [*Drawing his sword*]—and ask the gentleman, whether he will resign the lady, without forcing you to proceed against him?

Abso. Come then, sir [*Draws*]. Since you won't let it be an amicable suit, here's my reply.

Enter SIR ANTHONY, DAVID, *and* LADIES

David. Knock 'em all down, sweet Sir Anthony; knock down my master in particular and bind his hands over* to their good behaviour.

Sir Ant. Put up, Jack, put up, or I shall be in a frenzy— how came you in a duel, sir?

Abso. Faith, sir! that gentleman can tell you better than I; he called me out, without explaining his reasons.

Sir Ant. Sir, how came you to call my son out, without explaining your reasons?

Sir Luc. Your son, sir, insulted me in a manner which my honour could not brook.

Sir Ant. Jack, how durst you insult the gentleman in a manner which his honour could not brook?

Mrs. Mal. Come, come, let's have no honour before ladies. Captain Absolute, come here. How could you intimidate us so? Here's Lydia has just been terrified to death for you.

Abso. For fear I should be killed, or escape, ma'am?

Mrs. Mal. Nay, no delusions to the past—Lydia is convinced. Speak, child.

Sir Luc. With your leave, ma'am, I must put in a word here—I believe I could interpret the young lady's silence. Now mark——

Lyd. What is it you mean, sir?

Sir Luc. Come, come, Delia, we must be serious now—this is no time for trifling.

Lydia. 'T is true, sir: and your reproof bids me offer this gentleman my hand, and solicit the return of his affections.

Abso. Oh, my little angel, say you so?—Sir Lucius—I perceive there must be some mistake here, with regard to the affront which you say I have given you. I can only say that it could not have been intentional. And as you must be convinced, that I should not fear to support a real injury, you shall now see that I am not ashamed to atone for an inadvertency—I ask your pardon. But for this lady, while honoured with her approbation, I will support my claim against any man whatever.

Sir Ant. Well said, Jack, and I'll stand by you, my boy.

Acres. Mind, I give up all my claims—I make no pretensions to anything in the world—and if I can't get a wife without fighting for her, by my valour! I'll live a bachelor.

Sir Luc. Captain, give me your hand—an affront handsomely acknowledged becomes an obligation; and as for the lady—if she chooses to deny her own handwriting—here—— [*Takes out letters.*]

Mrs. Mal. Oh, he will dissolve my mystery! Sir Lucius, perhaps there's some mistake—perhaps I can illuminate——

Sir Luc. Pray, old gentlewoman, don't interfere where you have no business.—Miss Languish, are you my Delia or not?

Lyd. Indeed, Sir Lucius, I am not. [*Lydia and Absolute walk aside.*]

Mrs. Mal. Sir Lucius O'Trigger—ungrateful as you are—I own the soft impeachment—pardon my blushes, *I* am Delia.

Sir Luc. You, Delia, pho! pho! be easy.

Mrs. Mal. Why, thou barbarous Vandyke*—those letters are mine. When you are more sensible of my benignity, perhaps I may be brought to encourage your addresses.

Sir Luc. Mrs. Malaprop, I am extremely sensible of your condescension: and whether you or Lucy have put this trick upon me, I am equally beholden to you. And to show you I am not ungrateful, Captain Absolute, since you have taken that lady from me, I'll give you my Delia into the bargain.

Abso. I am much obliged to you, Sir Lucius: but here's my friend, Fighting Bob, unprovided for.

Sir Luc. Hah! little Valour, here will you make your fortune?

Acres. Odds wrinkles! No. But give me your hand, Sir Lucius, forget and forgive, but if ever I give you a chance of *pickling* me again, say Bob Acres is a dunce, that's all.

Sir Ant. Come, Mrs. Malaprop, don't be cast down—you are in your bloom yet. [*Seeing Julia and Faulkland engaged in earnest conversation*] What's going on here? So you have been quarrelling too, I warrant. Come Julia, I never interfered before : but let me have a hand in the matter at last. All the faults I have ever seen in my friend Faulkland, seemed to proceed from what he calls the delicacy and warmth of his affection for you. There, marry him directly. Julia, you'll find he'll mend surprisingly.

The rest come forward

Sir Luc. Come now, I hope there is no dissatisfied person but what is content? For as I have been disappointed myself, it will be very hard if I have not the satisfaction of seeing other people succeed better.

Acres. You are right, Sir Lucius—so, Jack, I wish you joy. Mr. Faulkland, the same. Ladies, come now, to show you I'm neither vexed nor angry, odds tabors and pipes! I'll order the fiddles in half an hour, to the New Rooms*, and I insist on you all meeting me there.

Sir Ant. Sir, I like your spirit : and at night we single lads will drink a health to the young couples, and a husband for Mrs. Malaprop.

CURTAIN

The School for Scandal

THE SCHOOL FOR SCANDAL

A COMEDY

DRAMATIS PERSONÆ

Sir Peter Teazle.
Sir Oliver Surface.
Sir Harry Bumper.
Sir Benjamin Backbite.
Joseph Surface.
Charles Surface.
Careless.
Snake.

Crabtree.
Rowley.
Moses.
Trip.
Lady Teazle.
Lady Sneerwell.
Mrs. Candour.
Maria.

Gentlemen, Maid, *and* Servants

SCENE—LONDON

ACT I

SCENE I.—LADY SNEERWELL'S *Dressing-room*

LADY SNEERWELL *discovered at her toilet;* SNAKE *drinking chocolate*

Lady Sneer. The paragraphs, you say, Mr. Snake, were all inserted.

Snake. They were, madam; and, as I copied them myself in a feigned hand, there can be no suspicion whence they came. In the common course of things, I think they must reach Mrs. Clackitt's ears within four-and-twenty hours; and then, you know, the business is as good as done.

Lady Sneer. Why, truly, Mrs. Clackitt has a very pretty talent, and a great deal of industry.

Snake. True, madam, and has been tolerably successful in her day. To my knowledge, she has been the cause of six matches being broken off, and three sons being disinherited. Nay, I have more than once traced her causing a *tête-à-tête* in the "Town and Country Magazine", when the parties, perhaps, had never seen each other's face before in the course of their lives.

Lady Sneer. She certainly has talents, but her manner is gross.

Snake. 'Tis very true. She generally designs well, has a free tongue and a bold invention; but her colouring is too dark, and her outlines often extravagant. She wants that delicacy of tint, and mellowness of sneer, which distinguish your ladyship's scandal.

Lady Sneer. You are partial*, Snake.

Snake. Not in the least; every body allows that Lady Sneerwell can do more with a word or look than many can with the most laboured detail, even when they happen to have a little truth on their side to support it.

Lady Sneer. Yes, my dear Snake; and I am no hypocrite to deny the satisfaction I reap from the success of my efforts. Wounded myself, in the early part of my life, by the envenomed tongue of slander, I confess I have since known no pleasure equal to the reducing others to the level of my own reputation.

Snake. Nothing can be more natural. But, Lady Sneerwell, there is one affair in which you have lately employed me, wherein, I confess, I am at a loss to guess your motives.

Lady Sneer. I conceive you mean with respect to my neighbour, Sir Peter Teazle, and his family?

Snake. I do. Here are two young men, to whom Sir Peter has acted as a kind of guardian since their father's death; the eldest possessing the most amiable character, and universally well spoken of—the youngest, the most dissipated and extravagant young fellow in the kingdom, without friends or character: the former an avowed admirer

---

* Throughout the text this mark is used to refer the reader to the notes.

of your ladyship, and apparently your favourite; the latter attached to Maria, Sir Peter's ward, and confessedly beloved by her. Now, on the face of these circumstances, it is utterly unaccountable to me, why you, the widow of a city knight, with a good jointure, should not close with the passion of a man of such character and expectations as Mr. Surface; and more so why you should be so uncommonly earnest to destroy the mutual attachment subsisting between his brother Charles and Maria.

Lady Sneer. Then, at once to unravel this mystery, I must inform you that love has no share whatever in the intercourse between Mr. Surface and me.

Snake. No!

Lady Sneer. His real attachment is to Maria, or her fortune; but, finding in his brother a favoured rival, he has been obliged to mask his pretensions, and profit by my assistance.

Snake. Yet still I am more puzzled why you should interest yourself in his success.

Lady Sneer. Heavens! how dull you are! Cannot you surmise the weakness which I hitherto, through shame, have concealed even from you? Must I confess that Charles —that libertine, that extravagant, that bankrupt in fortune and reputation—that he it is for whom I am thus anxious and malicious, and to gain whom I would sacrifice every thing?

Snake. Now, indeed, your conduct appears consistent: but how came you and Mr. Surface so confidential?

Lady Sneer. For our mutual interest. I have found him out a long time since. I know him to be artful, selfish, and malicious—in short, a sentimental knave; while with Sir Peter, and indeed with all his acquaintance, he passes for a youthful miracle of prudence, good sense, and benevolence.

Snake. Yes; yet Sir Peter vows he has not his equal in England; and, above all, he praises him as a man of sentiment.

Lady Sneer. True; and with the assistance of his sentiment and hypocrisy he has brought Sir Peter entirely into his interest with regard to Maria; while poor Charles has no friend in the house—though, I fear, he has a powerful one in Maria's heart, against whom we must direct our schemes.

Enter Servant

Ser. Mr. Surface.

Lady Sneer. Show him up. [*Exit Servant*

Enter JOSEPH SURFACE

Jos. Surf. My dear Lady Sneerwell, how do you do to-day? Mr. Snake, your most obedient.

Lady Sneer. Snake has just been rallying me on our mutual attachment: but I have informed him of our real views. You know how useful he has been to us; and, believe me, the confidence is not ill placed.

Jos. Surf. Madam, it is impossible for me to suspect a man of Mr. Snake's sensibility and discernment.

Lady Sneer. Well, well, no compliments now; but tell me when you saw your mistress, Maria — or, what is more material to me, your brother.

Jos. Surf. I have not seen either since I left you; but I can inform you that they never meet. Some of your stories have taken a good effect on Maria.

Lady Sneer. Ah, my dear Snake! the merit of this belongs to you. But do your brother's distresses increase?

Jos. Surf. Every hour. I am told he has had another execution in the house yesterday. In short, his dissipation and extravagance exceed any thing I ever heard of.

Lady Sneer. Poor Charles!

Jos. Surf. True, madam; notwithstanding his vices, one can't help feeling for him. Poor Charles! I'm sure I wish it were in my power to be of any essential service to him; for the man who does not share in the distresses of a brother, even though merited by his own misconduct, deserves——

Lady Sneer. O Lud! you are going to be moral, and forget that you are among friends.

Jos. Surf. Egad, that's true! I'll keep that sentiment till I see Sir Peter. However, it is certainly a charity to rescue Maria from such a libertine, who, if he is to be reclaimed, can be so only by a person of your ladyship's superior accomplishments and understanding.

Snake. I believe, Lady Sneerwell, here's company coming:

I'll go and copy the letter I mentioned to you.   Mr. Surface, your most obedient.

Jos. Surf. Sir, your very devoted.—[*Exit Snake.*]   Lady Sneerwell, I am very sorry you have put any farther confidence in that fellow.

Lady Sneer. Why so?

Jos. Surf. I have lately detected him in frequent conference with old Rowley, who was formerly my father's steward, and has never, you know, been a friend of mine.

Lady Sneer. And do you think he would betray us?

Jos. Surf. Nothing more likely: take my word for't, Lady Sneerwell, that fellow hasn't virtue enough to be faithful even to his own villany.   Ah, Maria!

Enter MARIA

Lady Sneer. Maria, my dear, how do you do?   What's the matter?

Mar. Oh! there's that disagreeable lover of mine, Sir Benjamin Backbite, has just called at my guardian's, with his odious uncle, Crabtree; so I slipped out, and ran hither to avoid them.

Lady Sneer. Is that all?

Jos. Surf. If my brother Charles had been of the party, madam, perhaps you would not have been so much alarmed.

Lady Sneer. Nay, now you are severe; for I dare swear the truth of the matter is, Maria heard you were here.   But, my dear, what has Sir Benjamin done, that you should avoid him so?

Mar. Oh, he has done nothing—but 'tis for what he has said: his conversation is a perpetual libel on all his acquaintance.

Jos. Surf. Ay, and the worst of it is, there is no advantage in not knowing him; for he'll abuse a stranger just as soon as his best friend: and his uncle's as bad.

Lady Sneer. Nay, but we should make allowance; Sir Benjamin is a wit and a poet.

Mar. For my part, I own, madam, wit loses its respect with me, when I see it in company with malice.   What do you think, Mr. Surface?

Jos. Surf. Certainly, madam; to smile at the jest which

plants a thorn in another's breast is to become a principal in the mischief.

Re-enter Servant

Ser. Madam, Mrs. Candour is below, and, if your lady-ship's at leisure, will leave her carriage.

Lady Sneer. Beg her to walk in.—[*Exit Servant.*] Now, Maria, here is a character to your taste; for, though Mrs. Candour is a little talkative, every body allows her to be the best natured and best sort of woman.

Mar. Yes, with a very gross affectation of good nature and benevolence, she does more mischief than the direct malice of old Crabtree.

Jos. Surf. I' faith that's true, Lady Sneerwell: whenever I hear the current running against the characters of my friends, I never think them in such danger as when Candour undertakes their defence.

Lady Sneer. Hush!—here she is!

Enter MRS. CANDOUR

Mrs. Can. My dear Lady Sneerwell, how have you been this century?—Mr. Surface, what news do you hear?—though indeed it is no matter, for I think one hears nothing else but scandal.

Jos. Surf. Just so, indeed, ma'am.

Mrs. Can. Oh, Maria! child,—what, is the whole affair off between you and Charles? His extravagance, I presume —the town talks of nothing else.

Mar. I am very sorry, ma'am, the town has so little to do.

Mrs. Can. True, true, child; but there's no stopping people's tongues. I own I was hurt to hear it, as I indeed was to learn, from the same quarter, that your guardian, Sir Peter, and Lady Teazle have not agreed lately as well as could be wished. But, Lord, do you think I would report these things! No, no! tale-bearers are just as bad as the tale-makers. By the by, Mr. Surface, I hope 'tis not true that your brother is absolutely ruined?

Jos. Surf. I am afraid his circumstances are very bad indeed, ma'am.

Mrs. Can. Ah! I heard so—but you must tell him to keep

up his spirits; every body almost is in the same way: Lord
Spindle, Sir Thomas Splint, Captain Quinze, and Mr. Nickit
—all up, I hear, within this week; so, if Charles is undone,
he'll find half his acquaintance ruined too, and that, you
know, is a consolation.

Jos. Surf. Doubtless, ma'am—a very great one.

Re-enter Servant

Ser. Mr. Crabtree and Sir Benjamin Backbite.   [*Exit*
Lady Sneer. So, Maria, you see your lover pursues you;
positively you sha'n't escape.

Enter CRABTREE *and* SIR BENJAMIN BACKBITE

Crab. Lady Sneerwell, I kiss your hand. Mrs. Candour,
I don't believe you are acquainted with my nephew, Sir
Benjamin Backbite? Egad, ma'am, he has a pretty wit,
and is a pretty poet too. Isn't he, Lady Sneerwell?

Sir Ben. Oh, fie, uncle!

Crab. Nay, egad it's true; I back him at a rebus* or a
charade against the best rhymer in the kingdom. Has your
ladyship heard the epigram he wrote last week on Lady
Frizzle's feather catching fire?—Do, Benjamin, repeat it.

Sir Ben. Uncle, now—pr'ythee——

Crab. I' faith, ma'am, 'twould surprise you to hear how
ready he is at all these sort of things.

Lady Sneer. I wonder, Sir Benjamin, you never publish
any thing.

Sir Ben. To say truth, ma'am, 'tis very vulgar to print;
and, as my little productions are mostly satires and lam-
poons* on particular people, I find they circulate more by
giving copies in confidence to the friends of the parties.
However, I have some love elegies, which, when favoured
with this lady's smiles, I mean to give the public.

[*Pointing to Maria*

Crab. [*To Maria*] 'Fore heaven, ma'am, they'll immor-
talize you! — you will be handed down to posterity, like
Petrarch's Laura*, or Waller's Sacharissa*.

Sir Ben. [*To Maria*] Yes, madam, I think you will like
them, when you shall see them on a beautiful quarto page,
where a neat rivulet of text shall meander through a meadow

of margin.   They will be the most elegant things of their kind!

Crab. Mr. Surface, pray is it true that your uncle, Sir Oliver, is coming home?

Jos. Surf. Not that I know of, indeed, sir.

Crab. He has been in the East Indies a long time.   You can scarcely remember him, I believe?   Sad comfort, whenever he returns, to hear how your brother has gone on!

Mar. [*Aside*] Their malice is intolerable!—[*Aloud*] Lady Sneerwell, I must wish you a good morning: I'm not very well.   [*Exit*

Mrs. Can. O dear! she changes colour very much.

Lady Sneer. Do, Mrs. Candour, follow her: she may want your assistance.

Mrs. Can. That I will, with all my soul, ma'am.   [*Exit*

Lady Sneer. 'Twas nothing but that she could not bear to hear Charles reflected on, notwithstanding their difference.

Sir Ben. The young lady's *penchant* is obvious.

Crab. But, Benjamin, you must not give up the pursuit for that: follow her, and put her into good humour.   Repeat her some of your own verses.   Come, I'll assist you.

Sir Ben. Mr. Surface, I did not mean to hurt **you**; but depend on't your brother is utterly undone.

Crab. O Lud, ay! undone as ever man was—can't raise a guinea.

Sir Ben. And every thing sold, I'm told, that was movable.

Crab. I have seen one that was at his house.   Not a thing left but some empty bottles that were overlooked, and the family pictures, which I believe are framed in the wainscots.

Sir Ben. And I'm very sorry also to hear some bad stories against him.   [*Going*

Crab. Oh, he has done many mean things, that's certain.

Sir Ben. But, however, as he's your brother——   [*Going*

Crab. We'll tell you all another opportunity.

                          [*Exeunt Crabtree and Sir Benjamin*

Lady Sneer. Ha ha! 'tis very hard for them to leave a subject they have not quite run down.

Jos. Surf. And I believe the abuse was no more acceptable to your ladyship than Maria.

Lady Sneer. I doubt her affections are farther engaged

than we imagine. But the family are to be here this evening, so you may as well dine where you are, and we shall have an opportunity of observing farther; in the meantime, I'll go and plot mischief, and you shall study sentiment.

[Exeunt

SCENE II.—*A Room in* SIR PETER TEAZLE'S *House*

Enter SIR PETER TEAZLE

Sir Pet. When an old bachelor marries a young wife, what is he to expect? 'Tis now six months since Lady Teazle made me the happiest of men—and I have been the most miserable dog ever since! We tift a little going to church, and fairly quarrelled before the bells had done ringing. I was more than once nearly choked with gall during the honeymoon, and had lost all comfort in life before my friends had done wishing me joy. Yet I chose with caution—a girl bred wholly in the country, who never knew luxury beyond one silk gown, nor dissipation above the annual gala of a race ball. Yet she now plays her part in all the extravagant fopperies of fashion and the town, with as ready a grace as if she never had seen a bush or a grass-plot out of Grosvenor Square! I am sneered at by all my acquaintance, and paragraphed in the newspapers. She dissipates my fortune, and contradicts all my humours; yet the worst of it is, I doubt I love her, or I should never bear all this. However, I'll never be weak enough to own it.

Enter ROWLEY

Row. Oh! Sir Peter, your servant: how is it with you, sir?

Sir Pet. Very bad, Master Rowley, very bad. I meet with nothing but crosses and vexations.

Row. What can have happened since yesterday?

Sir Pet. A good question to a married man!

Row. Nay, I'm sure, Sir Peter, your lady can't be the cause of your uneasiness.

Sir Pet. Why, has any body told you she was dead?

Row. Come, come, Sir Peter, you love her, notwithstanding your tempers don't exactly agree.

Sir Pet. But the fault is entirely hers, Master Rowley. I am, myself, the sweetest-tempered man alive, and hate a teasing temper; and so I tell her a hundred times a day.

Row. Indeed!

Sir Pet. Ay; and what is very extraordinary, in all our disputes she is always in the wrong! But Lady Sneerwell, and the set she meets at her house, encourage the perverseness of her disposition. Then, to complete my vexation, Maria, my ward, whom I ought to have the power of a father over, is determined to turn rebel too, and absolutely refuses the man whom I have long resolved on for her husband; meaning, I suppose, to bestow herself on his profligate brother.

Row. I am sorry to find you so violent against the young man, because this may be the most critical period of his fortune. I came hither with news that will surprise you.

Sir Pet. What! let me hear.

Row. Sir Oliver is arrived, and at this moment in town.

Sir Pet. How! you astonish me! I thought you did not expect him this month.

Row. I did not: but his passage has been remarkably quick.

Sir Pet. Egad, I shall rejoice to see my old friend. 'Tis sixteen years since we met. We have had many a day together:—but does he still enjoin us not to inform his nephews of his arrival?

Row. Most strictly. He means, before it is known, to make some trial of their dispositions.

Sir Pet. Ah! there needs no art to discover their merits—however, he shall have his way; but, pray, does he know I am married?

Row. Yes, and will soon wish you joy.

Sir Pet. What, as we drink health to a friend in a consumption! Ah! Oliver will laugh at me. We used to rail at matrimony together, but he has been steady to his text. Well, he must be soon at my house, though—I'll instantly give orders for his reception. But, Master Rowley, don't drop a word that Lady Teazle and I ever disagree.

Row. By no means.

Sir Pet. For I should never be able to stand Noll's jokes;

so I'll have him think, Lord forgive me! that we are a very happy couple.

Row. I understand you:—but then you must be very careful not to differ while he is in the house with you.

Sir Pet. Egad, and so we must—and that's impossible. Ah! Master Rowley, when an old bachelor marries a young wife, he deserves—to—the crime carries its punishment along with it.   [*Exeunt*

ACT II

Scene I.—*A Room in* Sir Peter Teazle's *House*

Enter Sir Peter *and* Lady Teazle

Sir Pet. Lady Teazle, Lady Teazle, I'll not bear it!

Lady Teaz. Sir Peter, Sir Peter, you may bear it or not, as you please; but I ought to have my own way in every thing, and, what's more, I will too. What! though I was educated in the country, I know very well that women of fashion in London are accountable to nobody after they are married.

Sir Pet. Very well, ma'am, very well; so a husband is to have no influence, no authority?

Lady Teaz. Authority! No, to be sure:—if you wanted authority over me, you should have adopted me, and not married me: I am sure you were old enough.

Sir Pet. Old enough!—ay, there it is. Well, well, Lady Teazle, though my life may be made unhappy by your temper, I'll not be ruined by your extravagance!

Lady Teaz. My extravagance! I'm sure I'm not more extravagant than a woman of fashion ought to be.

Sir Pet. No, no, madam, you shall throw away no more sums on such unmeaning luxury. 'Slife! to spend as much to furnish your dressing-room with flowers in winter as would suffice to turn the Pantheon* into a greenhouse, and give a *fête champêtre* at Christmas.

Lady Teaz. And am I to blame, Sir Peter, because flowers are dear in cold weather? You should find fault with the climate, and not with me. For my part, I'm sure I wish it was spring all the year round, and that roses grew under our feet!

Sir Pet. Oons! madam—if you had been born to this, I shouldn't wonder at your talking thus; but you forget what your situation was when I married you.

Lady Teaz. No, no, I don't; 'twas a very disagreeable one, or I should never have married you.

Sir Pet. Yes, yes, madam, you were then in somewhat a humbler style—the daughter of a plain country squire. Recollect, Lady Teazle, when I saw you first sitting at your tambour, in a pretty figured linen gown, with a bunch of keys at your side, your hair combed smooth over a roll, and your apartment hung round with fruits in worsted, of your own working.

Lady Teaz. Oh, yes! I remember it very well, and a curious life I led. My daily occupation to inspect the dairy, superintend the poultry, make extracts from the family receipt-book, and comb my aunt Deborah's lapdog.

Sir Pet. Yes, yes, ma'am, 'twas so indeed.

Lady Teaz. And then you know, my evening amusements! To draw patterns for ruffles, which I had not materials to make up; to play Pope Joan* with the curate; to read a sermon to my aunt; or to be stuck down to an old spinet to strum my father to sleep after a fox-chase.

Sir Pet. I am glad you have so good a memory. Yes, ma'am, these were the recreations I took you from; but now you must have your coach—*vis-à-vis*—and three powdered footmen before your chair; and, in the summer, a pair of white cats to draw you to Kensington Gardens*.

Lady Teaz. For my part, I should think you would like to have your wife thought a woman of taste.

Sir Pet. Ay—there again—taste! Zounds! madam, you had no taste when you married me!

Lady Teaz. That's very true, indeed, Sir Peter! and, after having married you, I should never pretend to taste again, I allow. But now, Sir Peter, since we have finished our daily jangle, I presume I may go to my engagement at Lady Sneerwell's.

Sir Pet. Ay, there's another precious circumstance—a charming set of acquaintance you have made there!

Lady Teaz. Nay, Sir Peter, they are all people of rank and fortune, and remarkably tenacious of reputation.

Sir Pet. Yes, egad, they are tenacious of reputation with a vengeance; for they don't choose any body should have a character but themselves! Such a crew! Ah! many a wretch has rid on a hurdle who has done less mischief than these utterers of forged tales, coiners of scandal, and clippers of reputation.

Lady Teaz. What, would you restrain the freedom of speech?

Sir Pet. Ah! they have made you just as bad as any one of the society.

Lady Teaz. Why, I believe I do bear a part with a tolerable grace.

Sir Pet. Grace indeed!

Lady Teaz. But I vow I bear no malice against the people I abuse: when I say an ill-natured thing, 'tis out of pure good humour; and I take it for granted they deal exactly in the same manner with me. But, Sir Peter, you know you promised to come to Lady Sneerwell's too.

Sir Pet. Well, well, I'll call in, just to look after my own character.

Lady Teaz. Then, indeed, you must make haste after me, or you'll be too late. So good by to ye.   [*Exit*

Sir Pet. So—I have gained much by my intended expostulation! Yet with what a charming air she contradicts every thing I say, and how pleasantly she shows her contempt for my authority! Well, though I can't make her love me, there is great satisfaction in quarrelling with her; and I think she never appears to such advantage as when she is doing every thing in her power to plague me. [*Exit*

SCENE II.—*A Room in* LADY SNEERWELL'S *House*

LADY SNEERWELL, MRS. CANDOUR, CRABTREE, SIR BENJAMIN BACKBITE, *and* JOSEPH SURFACE, *discovered*

Enter LADY TEAZLE *and* MARIA

Lady Sneer. Lady Teazle, I hope we shall see Sir Peter?

Lady Teaz. I believe he'll wait on your ladyship presently.

Lady Sneer. Maria, my love, you look grave. Come, you shall sit down to piquet with Mr. Surface.

Mar. I take very little pleasure in cards—however, I'll do as your ladyship pleases.

Lady Teaz. I am surprised Mr. Surface should sit down with her; I thought he would have embraced this opportunity of speaking to me before Sir Peter came.   [*Aside*

Mrs. Can. Now, I'll die; but you are so scandalous, I'll forswear your society.

Lady Teaz. What's the matter, Mrs. Candour?

Mrs. Can. They'll not allow our friend Miss Vermilion to be handsome.

Lady Sneer. Oh, surely she is a pretty woman.

Crab. I am very glad you think so, ma'am.

Mrs. Can. She has a charming fresh colour.

Lady Teaz. Yes, when it is fresh put on.

Mrs. Can. Oh, fie! I'll swear her colour is natural: I have seen it come and go!

Lady Teaz. I dare swear you have, ma'am: it goes off at night, and comes again in the morning.

Mrs. Can. Ha! ha! ha! Well, you make me laugh; but I vow I hate you for it. What do you think of Miss Simper?

Sir Ben. Why, she has very pretty teeth.

Lady Teaz. Yes; and on that account, when she is neither speaking nor laughing (which very seldom happens), she never absolutely shuts her mouth, but leaves it always on a-jar, as it were—thus.   [*Shows her teeth*

Mrs. Can. How can you be so ill-natured?

Lady Teaz. Nay, I allow even that's better than the pains Mrs. Prim takes to conceal her losses in front. She draws her mouth till it positively resembles the aperture of a poor's-box, and all her words appear to slide out edgewise, as it were—thus: *How do you do, madam?   Yes, madam.*

[*Mimics*

Lady Sneer. Very well, Lady Teazle; I see you can be a little severe.

Lady Teaz. In defence of a friend it is but justice. But here comes Sir Peter to spoil our pleasantry.

Enter SIR PETER TEAZLE

Sir Pet. Ladies, your most obedient.—[*Aside*] Mercy on me, here is the whole set! a character dead at every word, I suppose.

Mrs. Can. I am rejoiced you are come, Sir Peter. They have been so censorious—and Lady Teazle as bad as any one.

Sir Pet. That must be very distressing to you, indeed, Mrs. Candour.

Mrs. Can. For my part, I own I cannot bear to hear a friend ill spoken of.

Sir Pet. No, to be sure!

Sir Ben. Oh! you are of a moral turn. Mrs. Candour and I can sit for an hour and hear Lady Stucco talk sentiment.

Lady Teaz. Nay, I vow Lady Stucco is very well with the dessert after dinner; for she's just like the French fruit one cracks for mottoes—made up of paint and proverb.

Mrs. Can. Ha! ha! ha!

Sir Pet. Mercy on my life!—a person they dine with twice a week!   [*Aside*

Mrs. Can. Nay, but I vow you shall not carry the laugh off so—for give me leave to say, that Lady Stucco——

Sir Pet. Madam, madam, I beg your pardon—there's no stopping these good gentlemen's tongues. But when I tell you, Mrs. Candour, that the lady they are abusing is a particular friend of mine, I hope you'll not take her part.

Lady Sneer. Ha! ha! ha! well said, Sir Peter! but you are a cruel creature—too phlegmatic* yourself for a jest, and too peevish to allow wit in others.

Sir Pet. Ah, madam, true wit is more nearly allied to good nature than your ladyship is aware of.

Lady Teaz. True, Sir Peter: I believe they are so near akin that they can never be united.

Sir Ben. Or rather, suppose them man and wife, because one seldom sees them together.

Crab. Well, for my part, I believe there never was a scandalous tale without some foundation.

Lady Sneer. Come, ladies, shall we sit down to cards in the next room?

Enter Servant, who whispers SIR PETER

Sir Pet. I'll be with them directly.—[*Exit Servant.*] I'll get away unperceived.   [*Aside*

Lady Sneer. Sir Peter, you are not going to leave us?

Sir Pet. Your ladyship must excuse me; I'm called away by particular business. But I leave my character behind me.   [*Exit*

Sir Ben. Well—certainly, Lady Teazle, that lord of yours is a strange being: I could tell you some stories of him would make you laugh heartily if he were not your husband.

Lady Teaz. Oh, pray don't mind that; come, do let's hear them.   [*Exeunt all but Joseph Surface and Maria*

Jos. Surf. Maria, I see you have no satisfaction in this society.

Mar. How is it possible I should? If to raise malicious smiles at the infirmities or misfortunes of those who have never injured us be the province of wit or humour, Heaven grant me a double portion of dulness!

Jos. Surf. Yet they appear more ill-natured than they are; they have no malice at heart.

Mar. Then is their conduct still more contemptible; for, in my opinion, nothing could excuse the intemperance of their tongues but a natural and uncontrollable bitterness of mind.

Jos. Surf. Undoubtedly, madam; and it has always been a sentiment of mine, that to propagate a malicious truth wantonly is more despicable than to falsify from revenge. But can you, Maria, feel thus for others, and be unkind to me alone? Is hope to be denied the tenderest passion?

Mar. Why will you distress me by renewing this subject?

Jos. Surf. Ah, Maria! you would not treat me thus, and oppose your guardian, Sir Peter's will, but that I see that profligate Charles is still a favoured rival.

Mar. Ungenerously urged! But, whatever my sentiments are for that unfortunate young man, be assured I shall not feel more bound to give him up, because his distresses have lost him the regard even of a brother.

Jos. Surf. Nay, but, Maria, do not leave me with a frown: by all that's honest, I swear——   [*Kneels*

Re-enter LADY TEAZLE *behind*

[*Aside*] Gad's life, here's Lady Teazle.—[*Aloud to Maria*]
You must not—no, you shall not—for, though I have the
greatest regard for Lady Teazle——

Mar. Lady Teazle!

Jos. Surf. Yet were Sir Peter to suspect——

Lady Teaz. [*Coming forward*] What is this, pray? Does
he take her for me?—Child, you are wanted in the next room.
—[*Exit Maria.*] What is all this, pray?

Jos. Surf. Oh, the most unlucky circumstance in nature!
Maria has somehow suspected the tender concern I have for
your happiness, and threatened to acquaint Sir Peter with
her suspicions, and I was just endeavouring to reason with
her when you came in.

Lady Teaz. Indeed! but you seemed to adopt a very
tender mode of reasoning—do you usually argue on your
knees?

Jos. Surf. Oh, she's a child, and I thought a little bombast
—— But, Lady Teazle, when are you to give me your
judgment on my library, as you promised?

Lady Teaz. No, no; I begin to think it would be imprudent. But we shall be missed—let us join the company.

Jos. Surf. But we had best not return together.

Lady Teaz. Well, don't stay; for Maria sha'n't come to
hear any more of your reasoning, I promise you.   [*Exit*

Jos. Surf. A curious dilemma, truly, my politics have run
me into! I wanted, at first, only to ingratiate myself with
Lady Teazle, that she might not be my enemy with Maria;
and I have, I don't know how, become her serious lover.
Sincerely I begin to wish I had never made such a point of
gaining so very good a character, for it has led me into so
many cursed rogueries that I doubt I shall be exposed at
last.   [*Exit*

SCENE III.—*A Room in* SIR PETER TEAZLE'S *House*

Enter SIR OLIVER SURFACE *and* ROWLEY

Sir Oliv. Ha! ha! ha! so my old friend is married, hey?
—a young wife out of the country. Ha! ha! ha! that he

should have stood bluff to old bachelor so long, and sink into a husband at last!

Row. But you must not rally him on the subject, Sir Oliver; 'tis a tender point, I assure you, though he has been married only seven months.

Sir Oliv. Then he has been just half a year on the stool of repentance!—Poor Peter! But you say he has entirely given up Charles—never sees him, hey?

Row. His prejudice against him is astonishing, and I am sure greatly increased by a jealousy of him with Lady Teazle, which he has industriously been led into by a scandalous society in the neighbourhood, who have contributed not a little to Charles's ill name. Whereas the truth is, I believe, if the lady is partial to either of them, his brother is the favourite.

Sir Oliv. Ay, I know there are a set of malicious, prating, prudent gossips, both male and female, who murder characters to kill time, and will rob a young fellow of his good name before he has years to know the value of it. But I am not to be prejudiced against my nephew by such, I promise you!

Row. Sir, 'tis this resolution gives me assurance that Charles may yet be a credit to his family. But here comes Sir Peter.

Sir Oliv. Egad, so he does! Mercy on me, he's greatly altered, and seems to have a settled married look! One may read husband in his face at this distance!

Enter SIR PETER TEAZLE

Sir Pet. Ha! Sir Oliver—my old friend! Welcome to England a thousand times!

Sir Oliv. Thank you, thank you, Sir Peter! and i' faith I am glad to find you well, believe me!

Sir Pet. Oh! 'tis a long time since we met—fifteen years, I doubt, Sir Oliver, and many a cross accident in the time.

Sir Oliv. Ay, I have had my share. But, what! I find you are married, hey, my old boy? Well, well, it can't be helped; and so—I wish you joy with all my heart!

Sir Pet. Thank you, thank you, Sir Oliver.—Yes, I have entered into—the happy state; but we'll not talk of that now.

Sir Oliv. True, true, Sir Peter; old friends should not begin on grievances at first meeting. No, no, no.

Row. [*Aside to Sir Oliver*] Take care, pray, sir.

Sir Oliv. Well, so one of my nephews is a wild rogue, hey?

Sir Pet. Wild! Ah! my old friend, I grieve for your disappointment there; he's a lost young man, indeed. However, his brother will make you amends; Joseph is, indeed, what a youth should be—every body in the world speaks well of him.

Sir Oliv. I am sorry to hear it; he has too good a character to be an honest fellow. But, however, don't mistake me, Sir Peter; I don't mean to defend Charles's errors: but, before I form my judgment of either of them, I intend to make a trial of their hearts; and my friend Rowley and I have planned something for the purpose.

Row. And Sir Peter shall own for once he has been mistaken.

Sir Pet. Oh, my life on Joseph's honour!

Sir Oliv. Well—come, give us a bottle of good wine, we'll drink the lads' health, and tell you our scheme.

Sir Pet. Allons, then!

Sir Oliv. And don't, Sir Peter, be so severe against your old friend's son. Odds my life! I am not sorry that he has run out of the course a little: for my part, I hate to see prudence clinging to the green suckers of youth; 'tis like ivy round a sapling, and spoils the growth of the tree.

[*Exeunt*

ACT III

SCENE I.—*A Room in* SIR PETER TEAZLE'S *House*

Enter SIR PETER TEAZLE, SIR OLIVER SURFACE, *and* ROWLEY

Sir Pet. Well, then, we will see this fellow first, and have our wine afterwards. But how is this, Master Rowley? I don't see the jet of your scheme.

Row. Why, sir, this Mr. Stanley, whom I was speaking

of, is nearly related to them by their mother. He was once a merchant in Dublin, but has been ruined by a series of undeserved misfortunes. He has applied, by letter, since his confinement, both to Mr. Surface and Charles: from the former he has received nothing but evasive promises of future service, while Charles has done all that his extravagance has left him power to do; and he is, at this time, endeavouring to raise a sum of money, part of which, in the midst of his own distresses, I know he intends for the service of poor Stanley.

Sir Oliv. Ah! he is my brother's son.

Sir Pet. Well, but how is Sir Oliver personally to——

Row. Why, sir, I will inform Charles and his brother that Stanley has obtained permission to apply personally to his friends; and, as they have neither of them ever seen him, let Sir Oliver assume his character, and he will have a fair opportunity of judging, at least, of the benevolence of their dispositions: and believe me, sir, you will find in the youngest brother one who, in the midst of folly and dissipation, has, as our immortal bard* expresses it,—

> "a heart to pity, and a hand,
> Open as day, for melting charity".

Sir Pet. Psha! What signifies his having an open hand or purse either, when he has nothing left to give? Well, well, make the trial, if you please. But where is the fellow whom you brought for Sir Oliver to examine, relative to Charles's affairs?

Row. Below, waiting his commands, and no one can give him better intelligence.—This, Sir Oliver, is a friendly Jew, who, to do him justice, has done every thing in his power to bring your nephew to a proper sense of his extravagance.

Sir Pet. Pray let us have him in.

Row. Desire Mr. Moses to walk up stairs.

[*Calls to Servant*

Sir Pet. But, pray, why should you suppose he will speak the truth?

Row. Oh, I have convinced him that he has no chance of recovering certain sums advanced to Charles but through the bounty of Sir Oliver, who he knows is arrived; so that you may depend on his fidelity to his own interests. I have also another evidence in my power, one Snake, whom I have detected in a matter little short of forgery, and shall shortly produce to remove some of your prejudices, Sir Peter, relative to Charles and Lady Teazle.

Sir Pet. I have heard too much on that subject.

Row. Here comes the honest Israelite.

Enter MOSES

—This is Sir Oliver.

Sir Oliv. Sir, I understand you have lately had great dealings with my nephew Charles.

Mos. Yes, Sir Oliver, I have done all I could for him; but he was ruined before he came to me for assistance.

Sir Oliv. That was unlucky, truly; for you have had no opportunity of showing your talents.

Mos. None at all; I hadn't the pleasure of knowing his distresses till he was some thousands worse than nothing.

Sir Oliv. Unfortunate, indeed! But I suppose you have done all in your power for him, honest Moses?

Mos. Yes, he knows that. This very evening I was to have brought him a gentleman from the city, who does not know him, and will, I believe, advance him some money.

Sir Pet. What, one Charles has never had money from before?

Mos. Yes, Mr. Premium, of Crutched* Friars, formerly a broker.

Sir Pet. Egad, Sir Oliver, a thought strikes me!—Charles, you say, does not know Mr. Premium?

Mos. Not at all.

Sir Pet. Now then, Sir Oliver, you may have a better opportunity of satisfying yourself than by an old romancing tale of a poor relation: go with my friend Moses, and represent Premium, and then, I'll answer for it, you'll see your nephew in all his glory.

Sir Oliv. Egad, I like this idea better than the other, and I may visit Joseph afterwards as old Stanley. Well, but how must I talk? there's certainly some cant of usury and mode of treating that I ought to know.

Sir Pet. Oh, there's not much to learn. The great point,

as I take it, is to be exorbitant enough in your demands. Hey, Moses?

Mos. Yes, that's a very great point.

Sir Oliv. I'll answer for't I'll not be wanting in that. I'll ask him eight or ten per cent on the loan, at least.

Mos. If you ask him no more than that, you'll be discovered immediately.

Sir Oliv. Hey! what, the plague! how much then?

Mos. That depends upon the circumstances. If he appears not very anxious for the supply, you should require only forty or fifty per cent; but if you find him in great distress, and want the moneys very bad, you may ask double.

Sir Pet. A good honest trade you're learning, Sir Oliver!

Sir Oliv. So, so—Moses shall give me farther instructions as we go together.

Sir Pet. You will not have much time, for your nephew lives hard by.

Sir Oliv. Oh, never fear! my tutor appears so able, that though Charles lived in the next street, it must be my own fault if I am not a complete rogue before I turn the corner.

[*Exit with Moses*

Sir Pet. So, now, I think Sir Oliver will be convinced: you are partial, Rowley, and would have prepared Charles for the other plot.

Row. No, upon my word, Sir Peter.

Sir Pet. Well, go bring me this Snake, and I'll hear what he has to say presently. I see Maria, and want to speak with her.—[*Exit Rowley.*] I should be glad to be convinced my suspicions of Lady Teazle and Charles were unjust. I have never yet opened my mind on this subject to my friend Joseph—I am determined I will do it—he will give me his opinion sincerely.

Enter MARIA

So, child, has Mr. Surface returned with you?

Mar. No, sir; he was engaged.

Sir Pet. Well, Maria, do you not reflect, the more you converse with that amiable young man, what return his partiality for you deserves?

Mar. Indeed, Sir Peter, your frequent importunity on this

subject distresses me extremely—you compel me to declare, that I know no man who has ever paid me a particular attention whom I would not prefer to Mr. Surface.

Sir Pet. So—here's perverseness! No, no, Maria, 'tis Charles only whom you would prefer. 'Tis evident his vices and follies have won your heart.

Mar. This is unkind, sir.

Sir Pet. Go, perverse and obstinate! But take care, madam; you have never yet known what the authority of a guardian is: don't compel me to inform you of it.

Mar. I can only say, you shall not have just reason. 'Tis true, by my father's will, I am for a short period bound to regard you as his substitute; but must cease to think you so, when you would compel me to be miserable. [*Exit*

Sir Pet. Was ever man so crossed as I am, every thing conspiring to fret me! I had not been involved in matrimony a fortnight, before her father, a hale and hearty man, died, on purpose, I believe, for the pleasure of plaguing me with the care of his daughter.—[*Lady Teazle sings without.*] But here comes my helpmate! She appears in great good humour. How happy I should be if I could tease her into loving me, though but a little!

Enter LADY TEAZLE

Lady Teaz. Lud! Sir Peter, I hope you haven't been quarrelling with Maria? It is not using me well to be ill-humoured when I am not by.

Sir Pet. Ah, Lady Teazle, you might have the power to make me good-humoured at all times.

Lady Teaz. I am sure I wish I had; for I want you to be in a charming sweet temper at this moment. Do be good-humoured now, and let me have two hundred pounds, will you?

Sir Pet. Two hundred pounds; what, an't I to be in a good humour without paying for it? But speak to me thus, and i' faith there's nothing I could refuse you. You shall have it; but seal me a bond for the repayment.

Lady Teaz. Oh, no—there—my note of hand will do as well. [*Offering her hand*

Sir Pet. And you shall no longer reproach me with not

giving you an independent settlement. I mean shortly to surprise you : but shall we always live thus, hey?

Lady Teaz. If you please. I'm sure I don't care how soon we leave off quarrelling, provided you'll own you were tired first.

Sir Pet. Well—then let our future contest be, who shall be most obliging.

Lady Teaz. I assure you, Sir Peter, good nature becomes you. You look now as you did before we were married, when you used to walk with me under the elms, and tell me stories of what a gallant you were in your youth, and chuck me under the chin, you would ; and ask me if I thought I could love an old fellow, who would deny me nothing—didn't you?

Sir Pet. Yes, yes, and you were as kind and attentive——

Lady Teaz. And I dared say you'd make a very good sort of a husband.

Sir Pet. And you prophesied right; and we shall now be the happiest couple——

Lady Teaz. And never differ again?

Sir Pet. No, never!—though at the same time, indeed, my dear Lady Teazle, you must watch your temper very seriously; for in all our little quarrels, my dear, if you recollect, my love, you always began first.

Lady Teaz. I beg your pardon, my dear Sir Peter : indeed, you always gave the provocation.

Sir Pet. Now see, my angel! take care—contradicting isn't the way to keep friends.

Lady Teaz. Then don't you begin it, my love!

Sir Pet. There now! you—you are going on. You don't perceive, my life, that you are just doing the very thing which you know always makes me angry.

Lady Teaz. Nay, you know if you will be angry without any reason, my dear——

Sir Pet. There! now you want to quarrel again.

Lady Teaz. No, I'm sure I don't: but, if you will be so peevish——

Sir Pet. There now! who begins first?

Lady Teaz. Why, you, to be sure. I said nothing—but there's no bearing your temper.

Sir Pet. Now may all the plagues of marriage be doubled on me, if ever I try to be friends with you any more!

Lady Teaz. So much the better.

Sir Pet. No, no, madam: 'tis evident you never cared a pin for me, and I was a madman to marry you—a pert, rural coquette, that had refused half the honest 'squires in the neighbourhood!

Lady Teaz. And I am sure I was a fool to marry you— an old dangling bachelor, who was single at fifty, only because he never could meet with any one who would have him. Well, you are going to be in a passion, I see, and I shall only interrupt you—so, bye! bye!   [*Exit*

Sir Pet. Plagues and tortures! can't I make her angry either! Oh, I am the most miserable fellow! But I'll not bear her presuming to keep her temper: no! she may break my heart, but she sha'n't keep her temper.   [*Exit*

SCENE II.—*A Room in* CHARLES SURFACE'S *House*

CHARLES SURFACE, SIR HARRY BUMPER, CARELESS,
and Gentlemen, *discovered drinking*

Chas. Surf. But now, Sir Harry, beware, we must have beauty superlative.

Care. Nay, never study, Sir Harry: we'll stand to the toast, though your mistress should want an eye, and you know you have a song will excuse you.

Sir Har. Egad, so I have! and I'll give him the song instead of the lady.   [*Sings*

> Here's to the maiden of bashful fifteen;
>   Here's to the widow of fifty;
> Here's to the flaunting extravagant quean,
>   And here's to the housewife that's thrifty.
>
>   *Chorus.*   Let the toast pass,—
>   Drink to the lass,
> I'll warrant she'll prove an excuse for the glass.
>
> Here's to the charmer whose dimples we prize;
>   Now to the maid who has none, sir;
> Here's to the girl with a pair of blue eyes,
>   And here's to the nymph with but one, sir.
>
>   *Chorus.*   Let the toast pass, &c.

Here's to the maid with a bosom of snow:
    Now to her that's as brown as a berry:
Here's to the wife with a face full of woe,
    And now to the damsel that's merry.

Chorus.   Let the toast pass, &c.

For let 'em be clumsy, or let 'em be slim,
    Young or ancient, I care not a feather;
So fill a pint bumper quite up to the brim,
So fill up your glasses, nay, fill to the brim,
    And let us e'en toast them together.

Chorus.   Let the toast pass,—
        Drink to the lass,
I'll warrant she'll prove an excuse for the glass.

All. Bravo! bravo!

Enter TRIP, *and whispers* CHARLES SURFACE

Chas. Surf. Gentlemen, you must excuse me a little.—Careless, take the chair, will you?

Care. Nay, pr'ythee, Charles, what now? This is one of your peerless beauties, I suppose, has dropped in by chance?

Chas. Surf. No, faith! To tell you the truth, 'tis a Jew and a broker, who are come by appointment.

Care. Oh, let's have the Jew in.

1 *Gent.* Ay, and the broker too, by all means.

2 *Gent.* Yes, yes, the Jew and the broker.

Chas. Surf. Egad, with all my heart!—Trip, bid the gentlemen walk in.—[*Exit Trip.*] Though there's one of them a stranger, I can tell you.

Care. Charles, let us give them some generous Burgundy, and perhaps they'll grow conscientious.

Chas. Surf. Oh, hang 'em, no! wine does but draw forth a man's natural qualities; and to make them drink would only be to whet their knavery.

Care. Plague on 'em then! if they mayn't drink, we'll not sit down with them. Come, Harry, the dice are in the next room.—Charles, you'll join us when you have finished your business with the gentlemen?

Chas. Surf. I will! I will!—[*Exeunt Sir Harry Bumper and Gentlemen; Careless following.*]　Careless!

Care. [*Returning*] Well!

Chas. Surf. Perhaps I may want you.

Care. Oh, you know I am always ready: word, note, or bond, 'tis all the same to me.　　　　　　　[*Exit*

Re-enter TRIP, *with* SIR OLIVER SURFACE *and* MOSES

Mos. Sir, this is Mr. Premium, a gentleman of the strictest honour and secrecy; and always performs what he undertakes. Mr. Premium, this is——

Chas. Surf. Psha! have done. Sir, my friend Moses is a very honest fellow, but a little slow at expression: he'll be an hour giving us our titles. Mr. Premium, the plain state of the matter is this: I am an extravagant young fellow who wants to borrow money; you I take to be a prudent old fellow, who have got money to lend. I am blockhead enough to give fifty per cent sooner than not have it; and you, I presume, are rogue enough to take a hundred if you can get it. Now, sir, you see we are acquainted at once, and may proceed to business without farther ceremony.

Sir Oliv. Exceeding frank, upon my word. I see, sir, you are not a man of many compliments.

Chas. Surf. Oh, no, sir! plain dealing in business I always think best.

Sir Oliv. Sir, I like you the better for it. However, you are mistaken in one thing; I have no money to lend, but I believe I could procure some of a friend; but then he's an unconscionable dog. Isn't he, Moses? And must sell stock to accommodate you. Mustn't he, Moses?

Mos. Yes, indeed! You know I always speak the truth, and scorn to tell a lie!

Chas. Surf. Right. People that speak truth generally do. But these are trifles, Mr. Premium. What! I know money isn't to be bought without paying for't!

Sir Oliv. Well, but what security could you give? You have no land, I suppose?

Chas. Surf. Not a mole-hill, nor a twig, but what's in the bough-pots out of the window!

Sir Oliv. Nor any stock, I presume?

Chas. Surf. Nothing but live stock—and that's only a few pointers and ponies.   But pray, Mr. Premium, are you acquainted at all with any of my connexions?

Sir Oliv. Why, to say truth, I am.

Chas. Surf. Then you must know that I have a devilish rich uncle in the East Indies, Sir Oliver Surface, from whom I have the greatest expectations?

Sir Oliv. That you have a wealthy uncle, I have heard; but how your expectations will turn out is more, I believe, than you can tell.

Chas. Surf. Oh, no!—there can be no doubt.   They tell me I'm a prodigious favourite, and that he talks of leaving me every thing.

Sir Oliv. Indeed! this is the first I've heard of it.

Chas. Surf. Now I propose, Mr. Premium, if it's agreeable to you, a post-obit* on Sir Oliver's life: though at the same time the old fellow has been so liberal to me, that I give you my word, I should be very sorry to hear that any thing had happened to him.

Sir Oliv. Not more than I should, I assure you.   But the bond you mention happens to be just the worst security you could offer me—for I might live to a hundred and never see the principal.

Chas. Surf. Oh, yes, you would! the moment Sir Oliver dies, you know, you would come on me for the money.

Sir Oliv. Then I believe I should be the most unwelcome dun you ever had in your life.

Chas. Surf. What! I suppose you're afraid that Sir Oliver is too good a life?

Sir Oliv. No, indeed I am not; though I have heard he is as hale and healthy as any man of his years in Christendom.

Chas. Surf. There again, now, you are misinformed.   No, no, the climate has hurt him considerably, poor uncle Oliver. Yes, yes, he breaks apace, I'm told—and is so much altered lately that his nearest relations would not know him.

Sir Oliv. No! Ha! ha! ha! so much altered lately that his nearest relations would not know him!   Ha! ha! ha! egad—ha! ha! ha!

Chas. Surf. Ha! ha!—you're glad to hear that, little Premium?

Sir Oliv. No, no, I'm not.

Chas. Surf. Yes, yes, you are—ha! ha! ha!—you know that mends your chance.

Sir Oliv. But, sir, as I understand you want a few hundreds immediately, is there nothing you could dispose of?

Chas. Surf. How do you mean?

Sir Oliv. For instance, now, I have heard that your father left behind him a great quantity of massy old plate.

Chas. Surf. O Lud! that's gone long ago.   Moses can tell you how better than I can.

Sir Oliv. [*Aside*] Good lack! all the family race-cups and corporation-bowls!—[*Aloud*] Then it was also supposed that his library was one of the most valuable and compact.

Chas. Surf. Yes, yes, so it was—vastly too much so for a private gentleman.   For my part, I was always of a communicative disposition, so I thought it a shame to keep so much knowledge to myself.

Sir Oliv. [*Aside*] Mercy upon me! learning that had run in the family like an heir-loom!—[*Aloud*] Pray, what are become of the books?

Chas. Surf. You must inquire of the auctioneer, Master Premium, for I don't believe even Moses can direct you.

Mos. I know nothing of books.

Sir Oliv. So, so, nothing of the family property left, I suppose?

Chas. Surf. Not much, indeed; unless you have a mind to the family pictures.   I have got a room full of ancestors above; and if you have a taste for old paintings, egad, you shall have 'em a bargain!

Sir Oliv. Hey! what the devil! sure, you wouldn't sell your forefathers, would you?

Chas. Surf. Every man of them, to the best bidder.

Sir Oliv. What! your great-uncles and aunts?

Chas. Surf. Ay, and my great-grandfathers and grand-mothers too.

Sir Oliv. [*Aside*] Now I give him up!—[*Aloud*] What the plague, have you no bowels for your own kindred? Odd's

life! do you take me for Shylock* in the play, that you
would raise money of me on your own flesh and blood?

Chas. Surf. Nay, my little broker, don't be angry: what
need you care, if you have your money's worth?

Sir Oliv. Well, I'll be the purchaser: I think I can dispose of the family canvas.—[*Aside*] Oh, I'll never forgive
him this! never!

Re-enter CARELESS

Care. Come, Charles, what keeps you?

Chas. Surf. I can't come yet. I' faith, we are going to
have a sale above stairs; here's little Premium will buy all
my ancestors!

Care. Oh, burn your ancestors!

Chas. Surf. No, he may do that afterwards, if he pleases.
Stay, Careless, we want you: egad, you shall be auctioneer
—so come along with us.

Care. Oh, have with you, if that's the case. I can handle
a hammer as well as a dice-box! Going! going!

Sir Oliv. Oh, the profligates!   [*Aside*

Chas. Surf. Come, Moses, you shall be appraiser, if we
want one. Gad's life, little Premium, you don't seem to like
the business?

Sir Oliv. Oh, yes, I do, vastly! Ha! ha! ha! yes, yes,
I think it a rare joke to sell one's family by auction—ha! ha!
—[*Aside*] Oh, the prodigal!

Chas. Surf. To be sure! when a man wants money, where
the plague should he get assistance, if he can't make free
with his own relations?   [*Exeunt*

Sir Oliv. I'll never forgive him; never! never!

————————

ACT IV

SCENE I.—*A Picture Room in* CHARLES
SURFACE'S *House*

Enter CHARLES SURFACE, SIR OLIVER SURFACE,
MOSES, *and* CARELESS

Chas. Surf. Walk in, gentlemen, pray walk in;—here they
are, the family of the Surfaces, up to the Conquest.

Sir Oliv. And, in my opinion, a goodly collection.

Chas. Surf. Ay, ay, these are done in the true spirit of portrait-painting; no *volontière grace* or expression. Not like the works of your modern Raphaels*, who give you the strongest resemblance, yet contrive to make your portrait independent of you; so that you may sink the original and not hurt the picture. No, no; the merit of these is the inveterate likeness—all stiff and awkward as the originals, and like nothing in human nature besides.

Sir Oliv. Ah! we shall never see such figures of men again.

Chas. Surf. I hope not. Well, you see, Master Premium, what a domestic character I am; here I sit of an evening surrounded by my family. But come, get to your pulpit, Mr. Auctioneer; here's an old gouty chair of my grandfather's will answer the purpose.

Care. Ay, ay, this will do. Come, begin—A-going, a-going, a-going!

Chas. Surf. Bravo, Careless! Well, here's my great-uncle, Sir Richard Raveline, a marvellous good general in his day, I assure you. He served in all the Duke of Marlborough's wars, and got that cut over his eye at the battle of Malplaquet*. What say you, Mr. Premium? look at him—there's a hero! not cut out of his feathers, as your modern clipped captains are, but enveloped in wig and regimentals, as a general should be. What do you bid?

Sir Oliv. [*Aside to Moses*] Bid him speak.

Mos. Mr. Premium would have you speak.

Chas. Surf Why, then, he shall have him for ten pounds, and I'm sure that's not dear for a staff-officer.

Sir Oliv. [*Aside*] Heaven deliver me! his famous uncle Richard for ten pounds!—[*Aloud*] Very well, sir, I take him at that.

Chas. Surf. Careless, knock down my uncle Richard.—Here, now, is a maiden sister of his, my great-aunt Deborah, done by Kneller*, in his best manner, and esteemed a very formidable likeness. There she is, you see, a shepherdess feeding her flock. You shall have her for five pounds ten—the sheep are worth the money.

Sir Oliv. [*Aside*] Ah! poor Deborah! a woman who set

such a value on herself!—[*Aloud*] Five pounds ten—she's mine.

Chas. Surf. Knock down my aunt Deborah! This, now, is a grandfather of my mother's, a learned judge, well known on the western circuit.—What do you rate him at, Moses?

Mos. Four guineas.

Chas. Surf. Four guineas! Gad's life, you don't bid me the price of his wig.—Mr. Premium, you have more respect for the woolsack; do let us knock his lordship down at fifteen.

Sir Oliv. By all means.

Care. Gone!

Chas. Surf. Here's a jolly fellow—I don't know what relation, but he was mayor of Norwich: take him at eight pounds.

Sir Oliv. No, no; six will do for the mayor.

Chas. Surf. Come, make it guineas, and I'll throw you the two aldermen there into the bargain.

Sir Oliv. They're mine.

Chas. Surf. Careless, knock down the mayor and aldermen. But, plague on't! we shall be all day retailing in this manner; do let us deal wholesale: what say you, little Premium? Give me three hundred pounds for the rest of the family in the lump.

Care. Ay, ay, that will be the best way.

Sir Oliv. Well, well, any thing to accommodate you; they are mine. But there is one portrait which you have always passed over.

Care. What, that ill-looking little fellow over the settee?

Sir Oliv. Yes, sir, I mean that: though I don't think him so ill-looking a little fellow, by any means.

Chas. Surf. What, that? Oh; that's my uncle Oliver! 'twas done before he went to India.

Sir Oliv. But I suppose uncle Oliver goes with the rest of the lumber?

Chas. Surf. No, hang it! I'll not part with poor Noll. The old fellow has been very good to me, and, egad, I'll keep his picture while I've a room to put it in.

Sir Oliv. [*Aside*] The rogue's my nephew after all!— [*Aloud*] But, sir, I have somehow taken a fancy to that picture.

Chas. Surf. I'm sorry for't, for you certainly will not have it. Oons, haven't you got enough of them?

Sir Oliv. [*Aside*] I forgive him every thing!—[*Aloud*] But, sir, when I take a whim in my head, I don't value money. I'll give you as much for that as for all the rest.

Chas. Surf. Don't tease me, master broker; I tell you I'll not part with it, and there's an end of it.

Sir Oliv. [*Aside*] How like his father the dog is!— [*Aloud*] Well, well, I have done.—[*Aside*] I did not perceive it before, but I think I never saw such a striking resemblance.—[*Aloud*] Here is a draught for your sum.

Chas. Surf. Why, 'tis for eight hundred pounds!

Sir Oliv. You will not let Sir Oliver go?

Chas. Surf. Zounds! no! I tell you, once more.

Sir Oliv. Then never mind the difference, we'll balance that another time. But give me your hand on the bargain; you are an honest fellow, Charles—I beg pardon, sir, for being so free.—Come, Moses.   [*Exit with Moses*

Chas. Surf. So! this was an odd old fellow, indeed. Let me see, two-thirds of these five hundred and thirty odd pounds are mine by right. 'Fore Heaven! I find one's ancestors are more valuable relations than I took them for! —Ladies and gentlemen, your most obedient and very grateful servant.   [*Bows ceremoniously to the pictures, and exit*

SCENE II.—*Another Room in the same*

Enter SIR OLIVER SURFACE *and* MOSES

Mos. Well, sir, I think, as Sir Peter said, you have seen Mr. Charles in high glory; 'tis great pity he's so extravagant.

Sir Oliv. True, but he would not sell my picture.

Mos. And loves wine so much.

Sir Oliv. But he would not sell my picture.

Mos. And games so deep.

Sir Oliv. But he would not sell my picture. Oh, here's Rowley.

Enter ROWLEY

Row. So, Sir Oliver, I find you have made a purchase——

Sir Oliv. Yes, yes, our young rake has parted with his ancestors like old tapestry.

Row. And here has he commissioned me to re-deliver you part of the purchase money—I mean, though, in your necessitous character of old Stanley.

Mos. Ah! there is the pity of all; he is so charitable.

Row. And I left a hosier and two tailors in the hall, who, I'm sure, won't be paid, and this hundred would satisfy them.

Sir Oliv. Well, well, I'll pay his debts, and his benevolence too. But now I am no more a broker, and you shall introduce me to the elder brother as old Stanley.

Row. Not yet awhile; Sir Peter, I know, means to call there about this time.

SCENE III.—*A Library in* JOSEPH SURFACE'S *House*

Enter JOSEPH SURFACE *and Servant*

Jos. Surf. No letter from Lady Teazle?

Ser. No, sir.

Jos. Surf. [*Aside*] I am surprised she has not sent, if she is prevented from coming. Sir Peter certainly does not suspect me. Yet I wish I may not lose the heiress, through the scrape I have drawn myself into with the wife; however, Charles's imprudence and bad character are great points in my favour.   [*Knocking without*

Ser. Sir, I believe that must be Lady Teazle.

Jos. Surf. Hold! See whether it is or not, before you go to the door: I have a particular message for you if it should be my brother.

Ser. 'Tis her ladyship, sir; she always leaves her chair at the milliner's in the next street.

Jos. Surf. Stay, stay; draw that screen before the window —that will do;—my opposite neighbour is a maiden lady of so curious a temper.—[*Servant draws the screen, and exit.*] I have a difficult hand to play in this affair. Lady Teazle has lately suspected my views on Maria; but she must by no means be let into that secret,—at least, till I have her more in my power.

Enter LADY TEAZLE

Lady Teaz. What, sentiment in soliloquy now? Have you been very impatient? O Lud! don't pretend to look grave. I vow I couldn't come before.

Jos. Surf. O madam, punctuality is a species of constancy very unfashionable in a lady of quality.

[*Places chairs, and sits after Lady Teazle is seated*

Lady Teaz. Upon my word, you ought to pity me. Do you know Sir Peter is grown so ill-natured to me of late, and so jealous of Charles too—that's the best of the story, isn't it?

Jos. Surf. I am glad my scandalous friends keep that up.

[*Aside*

Lady Teaz. I am sure I wish he would let Maria marry him, and then perhaps he would be convinced; don't you, Mr. Surface?

Jos. Surf. [*Aside*] Indeed I do not.—[*Aloud*] Oh, certainly I do! for then my dear Lady Teazle would also be convinced how wrong her suspicions were of my having any design on the silly girl.

Lady Teaz. Well, well, I'm inclined to believe you. But isn't it provoking, to have the most ill-natured things said of one? And there's my friend Lady Sneerwell has circulated I don't know how many scandalous tales of me, who never say an ill-natured thing of any body—that is, of any friend; and then Sir Peter, too, to have him so peevish, and so suspicious, when I know the integrity of my own heart—indeed 'tis monstrous!

Jos. Surf. But, my dear Lady Teazle, 'tis your own fault if you suffer it. When a husband entertains a groundless suspicion of his wife, and withdraws his confidence from her, the original compact is broken, and she owes it to the honour of her sex to endeavour to outwit him.

Lady Teaz. Indeed! Do you think so? Why, if my understanding were once convinced——

Jos. Surf. Oh, certainly, madam, your understanding should be convinced. Yes, yes—Heaven forbid I should persuade you to do any thing you thought wrong. No, no, I have too much honour to desire it.

Lady Teaz. Don't you think we may as well leave honour out of the argument?   [*Rises*

Jos. Surf. Ah, the ill effects of your country education, I see, still remain with you.

Lady Teaz. I doubt they do indeed; and I will fairly own

to you, that if I could be persuaded, it would be by Sir Peter's ill usage sooner than your honourable logic, after all.

Jos. Surf. Then, by this hand, which he is unworthy of——
                                    [*Taking her hand*

Re-enter Servant

'Sdeath, you blockhead—what do you want?

Ser. I beg your pardon, sir, but I thought you would not choose Sir Peter to come up without announcing him.

Jos. Surf. Sir Peter!

Lady Teaz. Sir Peter! O Lud! I'm ruined! I'm ruined!

Ser. Sir, 'twasn't I let him in.

Lady Teaz. Oh! I'm quite undone! What will become of me? Now, Mr. Logic—Oh! mercy, sir, he's on the stairs—I'll get behind here—and if ever I'm so imprudent again——
                                    [*Goes behind the screen*

Jos. Surf. Give me that book.
                    [*Sits down. Servant pretends to adjust his chair*

Enter Sir Peter Teazle

Sir Pet. Ay, ever improving himself—Mr. Surface, Mr. Surface——   [*Pats Joseph on the shoulder*

Jos. Surf. Oh, my dear Sir Peter, I beg your pardon.—[*Gaping, throws away the book.*] I have been dozing over a stupid book. Well, I am much obliged to you for this call. You haven't been here, I believe, since I fitted up this room. Books, you know, are the only things I am a coxcomb in.

Sir Pet. 'Tis very neat indeed. Well, well, that's proper; and you can make even your screen a source of knowledge—hung, I perceive, with maps.

Jos. Surf. Oh, yes, I find great use in that screen.

Sir Pet. I dare say you must, certainly, when you want to find any thing in a hurry.

Jos. Surf. Ay, or to hide any thing in a hurry either.
                                    [*Aside*

Sir Pet. Well, I have a little private business——

Jos. Surf. You need not stay.   [*To Servant*

Ser. No, sir.   [*Exit*

Jos. Surf. Here's a chair, Sir Peter—I beg——

Sir Pet. Well, now we are alone, there is a subject, my

dear friend, on which I wish to unburden my mind to you—
a point of the greatest moment to my peace; in short, my
good friend, Lady Teazle's conduct of late has made me very
unhappy.

Jos. Surf. Indeed! I am very sorry to hear it.

Sir Pet. Yes, 'tis but too plain she has not the least regard
for me; but, what's worse, I have pretty good authority to
suppose she has formed an attachment to another.

Jos. Surf. Indeed! you astonish me!

Sir Pet. Yes! and, between ourselves, I think I've discovered the person.

Jos. Surf. How! you alarm me exceedingly.

Sir Pet. Ay, my dear friend, I knew you would sympathise
with me!

Jos. Surf. Yes, believe me, Sir Peter, such a discovery
would hurt me just as much as it would you.

Sir Pet. I am convinced of it. Ah! It is a happiness to
have a friend whom we can trust even with one's family
secrets. But have you no guess who I mean?

Jos. Surf. I haven't the most distant idea. It can't be
Sir Benjamin Backbite!

Sir Pet. Oh, no! What say you to Charles?

Jos. Surf. My brother! impossible!

Sir Pet. Oh, my dear friend, the goodness of your own
heart misleads you. You judge of others by yourself.

Jos. Surf. Certainly, Sir Peter, the heart that is conscious
of its own integrity is ever slow to credit another's treachery.

Sir Pet. True; but your brother has no sentiment—you
never hear him talk so. And then again—that the nephew
of my old friend, Sir Oliver, should be the person to attempt
such a wrong, hurts me more nearly.

Jos. Surf. Ay, there's the point. When ingratitude barbs
the dart of injury, the wound has double danger in it.

Sir Pet. Ay—I, that was, in a manner, left his guardian;
in whose house he had been so often entertained; who never
in my life denied him—my advice!

Jos. Surf. Yet I cannot suspect Lady Teazle.

Sir Pet. I am sure I wish to think well of her, and to
remove all ground of quarrel between us. She has lately
reproached me more than once with having made no settle-

ment on her; and, in our last quarrel, she almost hinted that she should not break her heart if I was dead. Now, as we seem to differ in our ideas of expense, I have resolved she shall have her own way, and be her own mistress in that respect for the future; and, if I were to die, she will find I have not been inattentive to her interest while living. Here, my friend, are the drafts of two deeds, which I wish to have your opinion on. By one, she will enjoy eight hundred a year independent while I live; and, by the other, the bulk of my fortune at my death.

Jos. Surf. This conduct, Sir Peter, is indeed truly generous.

Sir Pet. Yes, I am determined she shall have no cause to complain, though I would not have her acquainted with the latter instance of my affection yet awhile.

Jos. Surf. Nor I, if I could help it.   [*Aside*

Sir Pet. And now, my dear friend, if you please, we will talk over the situation of your hopes with Maria.

Jos. Surf. [*Softly*] Oh, no, Sir Peter; another time, if you please.

Sir Pet. I am sensibly chagrined at the little progress you seem to make in her affections.

Jos. Surf. [*Softly*] I beg you will not mention it. What are my disappointments when your happiness is in debate! —[*Aside*] 'Sdeath, I shall be ruined every way!

Sir Pet. And though you are averse to my acquainting Lady Teazle with your passion, I'm sure she's not your enemy in the affair.

Jos. Surf. Pray, Sir Peter, now oblige me. I am really too much affected by the subject we have been speaking of to bestow a thought on my own concerns. The man who is entrusted with his friend's distresses can never——

Re-enter Servant

Well, sir?

Ser. Your brother, sir, is speaking to a gentleman in the street, and says he knows you are within.

Jos. Surf. 'Sdeath, blockhead, I'm not within—I'm out for the day.

Sir Pet. Stay—hold—a thought has struck me:—you shall be at home.

Jos. Surf. Well, well, let him up.—[*Exit Servant.*] He'll interrupt Sir Peter, however.   [*Aside*

Sir Pet. Now, my good friend, oblige me, I entreat you. Before Charles comes, let me conceal myself somewhere; then do you tax him on the point we have been talking, and his answer may satisfy me at once.

Jos. Surf. Oh, fie, Sir Peter! would you have me join in so mean a trick?—to trepan my brother too?

Sir Pet. Nay, you tell me you are sure he is innocent; if so, you do him the greatest service by giving him an opportunity to clear himself, and you will set my heart at rest. Come, you shall not refuse me: [*Going up,*] here, behind the screen will be—Hey! what! there seems to be one listener here already—I'll swear I saw a petticoat!

Jos. Surf. Ha! ha! ha! Hark'ee, 'tis a little French milliner, a silly rogue that plagues me; and on your coming, sir, she ran behind the screen.

Sir Pet. Ah, Joseph! Joseph! But, egad, she has overheard all I have been saying of my wife.

Jos. Surf. Oh, 'twill never go any farther, you may depend upon it!

Sir Pet. No! then, faith, let her hear it out.—Here's a closet will do as well.

Jos. Surf. Well, go in there. [*Sir Peter goes into the closet.*] A narrow escape, indeed! and a curious situation I'm in, to part man and wife in this manner.

Lady Teaz. [*Peeping*] Couldn't I steal off?

Jos. Surf. Keep close, my angel!

Sir Pet. [*Peeping*] Joseph, tax him home.

Jos. Surf. Back, my dear friend!

Lady Teaz. [*Peeping*] Couldn't you lock Sir Peter in?

Jos. Surf. Be still, my life!

Sir Pet. [*Peeping*] You're sure the little milliner won't blab?

Jos. Surf. In, in, my dear Sir Peter!—'Fore Gad, I wish I had a key to the door.

Enter CHARLES SURFACE

Chas. Surf. Holla! brother, what has been the matter? Your fellow would not let me up at first.

Jos. Surf. Nothing, brother, I assure you.

Chas. Surf. But what has made Sir Peter steal off? I thought he had been with you.

Jos. Surf. He was, brother; but, hearing you were coming, he did not choose to stay.

Chas. Surf. What! was the old gentleman afraid I wanted to borrow money of him?

Jos. Surf. No, sir: but I am sorry to find, Charles, you have lately given that worthy man grounds for great uneasiness.

Chas. Surf. Yes, they tell me I do that to a great many worthy men. But how so, pray?

Jos. Surf. To be plain with you, brother, he thinks you are endeavouring to gain Lady Teazle's affections from him.

Chas. Surf. Who, I? O Lud! not I, upon my word.— Ha! ha! ha! ha! so the old fellow has found out that he has got a young wife, has he?—or, what is worse, Lady Teazle has found out she has an old husband?

Jos. Surf. This is no subject to jest on, brother. He who can laugh——

Chas. Surf. True, true, as you were going to say—then, seriously, I never had the least idea of what you charge me with, upon my honour.

Jos. Surf. Well, it will give Sir Peter great satisfaction to hear this.   [*Raising his voice*

Chas. Surf. To be sure, I once thought the lady seemed to have taken a fancy to me; but, upon my soul, I never gave her the least encouragement. Besides, you know my attachment to Maria. But, brother, do you know now that you surprise me exceedingly, by naming me with Lady Teazle; for, i' faith, I always understood you were her favourite.

Jos. Surf. Oh, for shame, Charles! This retort is foolish.

Chas. Surf. Nay, I swear I have seen you exchange such significant glances——

Jos. Surf. Nay, nay, sir, this is no jest.

Chas. Surf. Egad, I'm serious! Don't you remember one day, when I called here——

Jos. Surf. Nay, pr'ythee, Charles——

Chas. Surf. And found you together——

Jos. Surf. Zounds, sir, I insist——

Chas. Surf. And another time when your servant——

Jos. Surf. Brother, brother, a word with you!—[*Aside*] Gad, I must stop him.

Chas. Surf. Informed, I say, that——

Jos. Surf. Hush! I beg your pardon, but Sir Peter has overheard all we have been saying. I knew you would clear yourself, or I should not have consented.

Chas. Surf. How, Sir Peter! Where is he?

Jos. Surf. Softly, there! [*Points to the closet*

Chas. Surf. Oh, 'fore Heaven, I'll have him out. Sir Peter, come forth!

Jos. Surf. No, no——

Chas. Surf. I say, Sir Peter, come into court.—[*Pulls in Sir Peter.*] What! my old guardian!—What! turn inquisitor, and take evidence incog.? Oh, fie! Oh, fie!

Sir Pet. Give me your hand, Charles—I believe I have suspected you wrongfully; but you mustn't be angry with Joseph—'twas my plan!

Chas. Surf. Indeed!

Sir Pet. But I acquit you. I promise you I don't think near so ill of you as I did: what I have heard has given me great satisfaction.

Chas. Surf. Egad, then, 'twas lucky you didn't hear any more. Wasn't it, Joseph?

Sir Pet. Ah! you would have retorted on him.

Chas. Surf. Ah, ay, that was a joke.

Sir Pet. Yes, yes, I know his honour too well.

Chas. Surf. But you might as well have suspected him as me in this matter, for all that. Mightn't he, Joseph?

Sir Pet. Well, well, I believe you.

Jos. Surf. Would they were both out of the room! [*Aside*

Sir Pet. And in future, perhaps, we may not be such strangers.

Re-enter Servant, and whispers JOSEPH SURFACE

Ser. Lady Sneerwell is below, and says she will come up.

Jos. Surf. Lady Sneerwell! she must not come here. [*Exit Servant.*] Gentlemen, I beg pardon—I must wait on you down stairs: here is a person come on particular business.

Chas. Surf. Well, you can see him in another room. Sir Peter and I have not met a long time, and I have something to say to him.

Jos. Surf. [*Aside*] They must not be left together. I'll send Lady Sneerwell away; [*aloud*] I'll return directly.

[*Exit Joseph Surface*

Sir Pet. Ah, Charles, if you associated more with your brother, one might indeed hope for your reformation. He is a man of sentiment. Well, there is nothing in the world so noble as a man of sentiment.

Chas. Surf. Oh, hang him! he's a very anchorite, a young hermit!

Sir Pet. Hark'ee—you must not abuse him: he may chance to hear of it again, I promise you.

Chas. Surf. Why, you won't tell him?

Sir Pet. No—but—this way.—[*Aside*] Egad, I'll tell him. —[*Aloud*] Hark'ee—have you a mind to have a good laugh at Joseph?

Chas. Surf. I should like it of all things.

Sir Pet. Then, i' faith, we will! I'll be quit with him for discovering me.   [*Whispers, pointing to screen*

Chas. Surf. Oh, egad, we'll have a peep.

Sir Pet. Not for the world!—Joseph will never forgive me.

Chas. Surf. I'll stand by you——

Sir Pet. Odds, here he is!

[*Charles Surface throws down the screen*

Re-enter JOSEPH SURFACE

Chas. Surf. Lady Teazle, by all that's wonderful!

Sir Pet. Lady Teazle, by all that's horrible!

Chas. Surf. Egad, you seem all to have been diverting yourselves here at hide and seek, and I don't see who is out of the secret. Shall I beg your ladyship to inform me? Not a word!—Brother, will you be pleased to explain this matter? What! is Morality dumb too?—Sir Peter, though I found you in the dark, perhaps you are not so now! All mute!—Well —though I can make nothing of the affair, I suppose you perfectly understand one another: so I'll leave you to yourselves.—[*Going*] Brother, I'm sorry to find you have given

that worthy man grounds for so much uneasiness.—Sir Peter!
there's nothing in the world so noble as a man of sentiment!

[*Exit*

Jos. Surf. Sir Peter—notwithstanding—I confess—that
appearances are against me—if you will afford me your
patience—I make no doubt—but I shall explain every thing
to your satisfaction.

Sir Pet. If you please, sir.

Jos. Surf. The fact is, sir, that Lady Teazle, knowing my
pretensions to your ward Maria—I say, sir, Lady Teazle,
being apprehensive of the jealousy of your temper—and
knowing my friendship to the family—she, sir, I say—called
here—in order that—I might explain these pretensions—but
on your coming—being apprehensive—as I said—of your
jealousy—she withdrew—and this, you may depend on it, is
the whole truth of the matter.

Sir Pet. A very clear account, upon my word; and I dare
swear the lady will vouch for every article of it.

Lady Teaz. For not one word of it, Sir Peter!

Sir Pet. How! don't you think it worth while to agree in
the lie?

Lady Teaz. There is not one syllable of truth in what that
gentleman has told you.

Sir Pet. I believe you, upon my soul, ma'am!

Jos. Surf. [*Aside to Lady Teazle*] 'Sdeath, madam, will
you betray me?

Lady Teaz. Good Mr. Hypocrite, by your leave, I'll speak
for myself.

Sir Pet. Ay, let her alone, sir; you'll find she'll make out
a better story than you, without prompting.

Lady Teaz. Hear me, Sir Peter!—I came here on no
matter relating to your ward, and even ignorant of this
gentleman's pretensions to her. But I came, induced by
his insidious arguments, to listen to his pretended passion.

Sir Pet. Now, I believe, the truth is coming, indeed!

Jos. Surf. The woman's mad!

Lady Teaz. No, sir; she has recovered her senses, and
your own arts have furnished her with the means.—Sir Peter,
I do not expect you to credit me—but the tenderness you ex-
pressed for me, when I am sure you could not think I was a

witness to it, has so penetrated to my heart, that had I left the place without the shame of this discovery, my future life should have spoken the sincerity of my gratitude. As for that smooth-tongued hypocrite, I behold him now in a light so truly despicable, that I shall never again respect myself for having listened to him. [*Exit*

Jos. Surf. Notwithstanding all this, Sir Peter, Heaven knows——

Sir Pet. That you are a villain! and so I leave you to your conscience.

Jos. Surf. You are too rash, Sir Peter; you shall hear me. The man who shuts out conviction by refusing to——

Sir Pet. Oh, hang your sentiments!

[*Exeunt Sir Peter and Joseph Surface, talking*

ACT V

Scene I.—*The Library in* Joseph Surface's *House*

Enter Joseph Surface *and Servant*

Jos. Surf. Mr. Stanley! and why should you think I would see him? you must know he comes to ask something.

Ser. Sir, I should not have let him in, but that Mr. Rowley came to the door with him.

Jos. Surf. Psha! blockhead! to suppose that I should now be in a temper to receive visits from poor relations!—Well, why don't you show the fellow up?

Ser. I will, sir.—Why, sir, it was not my fault that Sir Peter discovered my lady——

Jos. Surf. Go, fool!—[*Exit Servant.*] Sure Fortune never played a man of my policy such a trick before! My character with Sir Peter, my hopes with Maria, destroyed in a moment! I'm in a rare humour to listen to other people's distresses. I sha'n't be able to bestow even a benevolent sentiment on Stanley.—So! here he comes, and Rowley with him. I must try to recover myself, and put a little charity into my face, however. [*Exit*

Enter SIR OLIVER SURFACE *and* ROWLEY

Sir Oliv. What! does he avoid us? That was he, was it not?

Row. It was, sir. But I doubt you are come a little too abruptly. His nerves are so weak, that the sight of a poor relation may be too much for him. I should have gone first to break it to him.

Sir Oliv. Yet he has a string of charitable sentiments at his fingers' ends.

Row. Or, rather, at his tongue's end, Sir Oliver; for I believe there is no sentiment he has such faith in as that *Charity begins at home.*

Sir Oliv. And his, I presume, is of that domestic sort which never stirs abroad at all.

Row. I doubt you'll find it so;—but he's coming. I mustn't seem to interrupt you; and you know, immediately as you leave him, I come in to announce your arrival in your real character.

Sir Oliv. True; and afterwards you'll meet me at Sir Peter's.

Row. Without losing a moment.   [*Exit*

Sir Oliv. I don't like the complaisance of his features

Re-enter JOSEPH SURFACE

Jos. Surf. Sir, I beg you ten thousand pardons for keeping you a moment waiting.—Mr. Stanley, I presume.

Sir Oliv. At your service.

Jos. Surf. Sir, I beg you will do me the honour to sit down—I entreat you, sir.

Sir Oliv. Dear sir—there's no occasion.—[*Aside*] Too civil by half!

Jos. Surf. I have not the pleasure of knowing you, Mr. Stanley; but I am extremely happy to see you look so well. You were nearly related to my mother, I think, Mr. Stanley?

Sir Oliv. I was, sir; so nearly that my present poverty, I fear, may do discredit to her wealthy children, else I should not have presumed to trouble you.

Jos. Surf. Dear sir, there needs no apology;—he that is in distress, though a stranger, has a right to claim kindred with the wealthy. I am sure I wish I was one of that class, and had it in my power to offer you even a small relief.

Sir Oliv. If your uncle, Sir Oliver, were here, I should have a friend.

Jos. Surf. I wish he was, sir, with all my heart: you should not want an advocate with him, believe me, sir.

Sir Oliv. I should not need one—my distresses would recommend me. But I imagined his bounty would enable you to become the agent of his charity.

Jos. Surf. My dear sir, you were strangely misinformed. Sir Oliver is a worthy man, a very worthy man; but avarice, Mr. Stanley, is the vice of the age. I will tell you, my good sir, in confidence, what he has done for me has been a mere nothing; though people, I know, have thought otherwise, and, for my part, I never chose to contradict the report.

Sir Oliv. What! has he never transmitted you bullion—rupees—pagodas?

Jos. Surf. Oh, dear sir, nothing of the kind! No, no; a few presents now and then—china, shawls, congou tea, avadavats*, and Indian crackers — little more, believe me.

Sir Oliv. Here's gratitude for twelve thousand pounds! —Avadavats and Indian crackers!   [*Aside*

Jos. Surf. Then, my dear sir, you have heard, I doubt not, of the extravagance of my brother: there are very few would credit what I have done for that unfortunate young man.

Sir Oliv. Not I, for one!   [*Aside*

Jos. Surf. The sums I have lent him! Indeed I have been exceedingly to blame; it was an amiable weakness; however, I don't pretend to defend it—and now I feel doubly culpable, since it has deprived me of the pleasure of serving you, Mr. Stanley, as my heart dictates.

Sir Oliv. [*Aside*] Dissembler!—[*Aloud*] Then, sir, you can't assist me?

Jos. Surf. At present, it grieves me to say, I cannot; but, whenever I have the ability, you may depend upon hearing from me.

Sir Oliv. I am extremely sorry——

Jos. Surf. Not more than I, believe me; to pity, without

the power to relieve, is still more painful than to ask and be denied.

Sir Oliv. Kind sir, your most obedient humble servant.

Jos. Surf. You leave me deeply affected, Mr. Stanley.—William, be ready to open the door.   [*Calls to Servant*

Sir Oliv. Oh, dear sir, no ceremony.

Jos. Surf. Your very obedient.

Sir Oliv. Your most obsequious.

Jos. Surf. You may depend upon hearing from me, whenever I can be of service.

Sir Oliv. Sweet sir, you are too good!

Jos. Surf. In the meantime I wish you health and spirits.

Sir Oliv. Your ever grateful and perpetual humble servant.

Jos. Surf. Sir, yours as sincerely.

Sir Oliv. [*Aside*] Now I am satisfied.   [*Exit*

Jos. Surf. This is one bad effect of a good character; it invites application from the unfortunate, and there needs no small degree of address to gain the reputation of benevolence without incurring the expense.

Re-enter ROWLEY

Row. Mr. Surface, your servant: I was apprehensive of interrupting you, though my business demands immediate attention, as this note will inform you.

Jos. Surf. Always happy to see Mr. Rowley,—a rascal.—[*Aside. Reads the letter.*] Sir Oliver Surface!—My uncle arrived!

Row. He is, indeed: we have just parted—quite well, after a speedy voyage, and impatient to embrace his worthy nephew.

Jos. Surf. I am astonished!—William! stop Mr. Stanley, if he's not gone.   [*Calls to Servant*

Row. Oh! he's out of reach, I believe.

Jos. Surf. Why did you not let me know this when you came in together?

Row. I thought you had particular business. But I must be gone to inform your brother, and appoint him here to meet your uncle. He will be with you in a quarter of an hour.

Jos. Surf. So he says. Well, I am strangely overjoyed at

his coming.—[*Aside*] Never, to be sure, was any thing so unlucky!

Row. You will be delighted to see how well he looks.

Jos. Surf. Oh! I'm overjoyed to hear it.—[*Aside*] Just at this time!

Row. I'll tell him how impatiently you expect him.

Jos. Surf. Do, do; pray give my best duty and affection. Indeed, I cannot express the sensations I feel at the thought of seeing him.—[*Exit Rowley.*] Certainly his coming just at this time is the cruellest piece of ill fortune.   [*Exit*

SCENE II.—*A Room in* SIR PETER TEAZLE'S *House*

Enter SIR OLIVER SURFACE, SIR PETER TEAZLE, *and* ROWLEY

Sir Oliv. Well, Sir Peter, I have seen both my nephews in the manner we proposed.

Sir Pet. A precious couple they are!

Row. Yes, and Sir Oliver is convinced that your judgment was right, Sir Peter.

Sir Oliv. Yes, I find Joseph is indeed the man, after all.

Row. Ay, as Sir Peter says, he is a man of sentiment.

Sir Oliv. And acts up to the sentiments he professes.

Row. It certainly is edification to hear him talk.

Sir Oliv. Oh, he's a model for the young men of the age! —But how's this, Sir Peter? you don't join us in your friend Joseph's praise, as I expected.

Sir Pet. Sir Oliver, we live in a wicked world, and the fewer we praise the better.

Row. What! do you say so, Sir Peter, who were never mistaken in your life?

Sir Pet. Psha! plague on you both! I see by your sneering you have heard the whole affair. I shall go mad among you!

Row. Then to fret you no longer, Sir Peter, we are indeed acquainted with it all. I met Lady Teazle coming from Mr. Surface's so humbled, that she deigned to request me to be her advocate with you.

Sir Pet. And does Sir Oliver know all this?

Sir Oliv. Every circumstance. Oh, I have been vastly diverted with the story! ha! ha! ha!

Sir Pet. 'Twas very pleasant.

Sir Oliv. I never laughed more in my life, I assure you: ah! ah! ah!

Sir Pet. Oh, vastly diverting! ha! ha! ha!

Row. But I see Lady Teazle going towards the next room; I am sure you must desire a reconciliation as early as she does.

Sir Oliv. Perhaps my being here prevents her coming to you. Well, I'll leave honest Rowley to mediate between you; but he must bring you all presently to Mr. Surface's, where I am now returning, if not to reclaim a libertine, at least to expose hypocrisy.

Sir Pet. Ah, I'll be present at your discovering* yourself there with all my heart; though 'tis a vile unlucky place for discoveries.

Row. We'll follow.   [*Exit Sir Oliver Surface*

Sir Pet. She is not coming here, you see, Rowley.

Row. No, but she has left the door of that room open, you perceive. See, she is in tears.

Sir Pet. Certainly a little mortification appears very becoming in a wife. Don't you think it will do her good to let her pine a little?

Row. Oh, this is ungenerous in you!

Sir Pet. Well, I know not what to think. You remember the letter I found of hers evidently intended for Charles?

Row. A mere forgery, Sir Peter! laid in your way on purpose. This is one of the points which I intend Snake shall give you conviction of.

Sir Pet. I wish I were once satisfied of that. She looks this way. What a remarkably elegant turn of the head she has! Rowley, I'll go to her.

Row. Certainly.

Sir Pet. Though, when it is known that we are reconciled, people will laugh at me ten times more.

Row. Let them laugh, and retort their malice only by showing them you are happy in spite of it.

Sir Pet. I' faith, so I will! and, if I'm not mistaken, we may yet be the happiest couple in the country.

Row. Nay, Sir Peter, he who once lays aside suspicion——

Sir Pet. Hold, Master Rowley! if you have any regard for me, never let me hear you utter any thing like a sentiment: I have had enough of them to serve me the rest of my life.

[*Exeunt*

SCENE III.—*The Library in* JOSEPH SURFACE'S *House*

Enter JOSEPH SURFACE *and* LADY SNEERWELL

Lady Sneer. Impossible! Will not Sir Peter immediately be reconciled to Charles, and of course no longer oppose his union with Maria? The thought is distraction to me.

Jos. Surf. Can passion furnish a remedy?

Lady Sneer. No, nor cunning either. Oh, I was a fool, an idiot, to league with such a blunderer!

Jos. Surf. Sure, Lady Sneerwell, I am the greatest sufferer: yet you see I bear the accident with calmness.

Lady Sneer. Because the disappointment doesn't reach your heart; your interest only attached you to Maria. Had you felt for her what I have for that ungrateful libertine, neither your temper nor hypocrisy could prevent your showing the sharpness of your vexation.

Jos. Surf. Well, I admit I have been to blame. I confess I deviated from the direct road of wrong, but I don't think we're so totally defeated neither.

Lady Sneer. No!

Jos. Surf. You tell me you have made a trial of Snake since we met, and that you still believe him faithful to us?

Lady Sneer. I do believe so.

Jos. Surf. And that he has undertaken, should it be necessary, to swear and prove, that Charles is at this time contracted by vows and honours to your ladyship, which some of his former letters to you will serve to support?

Lady Sneer. This, indeed, might have assisted.

Jos. Surf. Come, come; it is not too late yet.—[*Knocking at the door.*] But hark! this is probably my uncle, Sir Oliver: retire to that room; we'll consult farther when he is gone.

Lady Sneer. Well, but if he should find you out too?

Jos. Surf. Oh, I have no fear of that. Sir Peter will hold his tongue for his own credit's sake—and you may depend on it I shall soon discover Sir Oliver's weak side!

Lady Sneer. I have no diffidence of your abilities: only be constant to one roguery at a time.

Jos. Surf. I will, I will!—[*Exit Lady Sneerwell.*] Well, at all events, my character is so much better than Charles's, that I certainly—hey!—what—this is not Sir Oliver, but old Stanley again. Plague on't that he should return to tease me just now! I shall have Sir Oliver come and find him here—and——

Enter SIR OLIVER SURFACE

Gad's life, Mr. Stanley, why have you come back to plague me at this time? You must not stay now, upon my word.

Sir Oliv. Sir, I hear your uncle Oliver is expected here, and though he has been so penurious to you, I'll try what he'll do for me.

Jos. Surf. Sir, 'tis impossible for you to stay now, so I must beg——Come any other time, and I promise you, you shall be assisted.

Sir Oliv. No: Sir Oliver and I must be acquainted.

Jos. Surf. Zounds, sir! then I insist on your quitting the room directly.

Sir Oliv. Nay, sir——

Jos. Surf. Sir, I insist on't!—Here, William! show this gentleman out. Since you compel me, sir, not one moment —this is such insolence. [*Going to push him out*

Enter CHARLES SURFACE

Chas. Surf. Heyday! what's the matter now? What, have you got hold of my little broker here? Zounds, brother, don't hurt little Premium. What's the matter, my little fellow?

Jos. Surf. So! he has been with you too, has he?

Chas. Surf. To be sure, he has. Why, he's as honest a little—— But sure, Joseph, you have not been borrowing money too, have you?

Jos. Surf. Borrowing! no! But, brother, you know we expect Sir Oliver here every——

Chas. Surf. O Gad, that's true! Noll mustn't find the little broker here, to be sure.

Jos. Surf. Yet Mr. Stanley insists——

Chas. Surf. Stanley! why, his name's Premium.

Jos. Surf. No, sir, Stanley.

Chas. Surf. No, no, Premium.

Jos. Surf. Well, no matter which—but——

Chas. Surf. Ay, ay, Stanley or Premium, 'tis the same thing, as you say; for I suppose he goes by half a hundred names, besides A. B. at the coffee-house*.   [*Knocking*

Jos. Surf. 'Sdeath! here's Sir Oliver at the door.—Now I beg, Mr. Stanley——

Chas. Surf. Ay, ay, and I beg, Mr. Premium——

Sir Oliv. Gentlemen——

Jos. Surf. Sir, by Heaven you shall go!

Chas. Surf. Ay, out with him, certainly!

Sir Oliv. This violence——

Jos. Surf. Sir, 'tis your own fault.

Chas. Surf. Out with him, to be sure.

[*Both forcing Sir Oliver out*

Enter SIR PETER *and* LADY TEAZLE, MARIA,
and ROWLEY

Sir Pet. My old friend, Sir Oliver—hey! What in the name of wonder—here are dutiful nephews—assault their uncle at a first visit!

Lady Teaz. Indeed, Sir Oliver, 'twas well we came in to rescue you.

Row. Truly it was; for I perceive, Sir Oliver, the character of old Stanley was no protection to you.

Sir Oliv. Nor of Premium either: the necessities of the former could not extort a shilling from that benevolent gentleman; and with the other I stood a chance of faring worse than my ancestors, and being knocked down without being bid for.

Jos. Surf. Charles!

Chas. Surf. Joseph!

Jos. Surf. 'Tis now complete!

Chas. Surf. Very.

Sir Oliv. Sir Peter, my friend, and Rowley too—look on that elder nephew of mine. You know what he has already received from my bounty; and you also know how gladly I would have regarded half my fortune as held in trust for him: judge then my disappointment in discovering him to be destitute of truth, charity, and gratitude.

Sir Pet. Sir Oliver, I should be more surprised at this declaration, if I had not myself found him to be mean, treacherous, and hypocritical.

Lady Teaz. And if the gentleman pleads not guilty to these, pray let him call me to his character.

Sir Pet. Then, I believe, we need add no more: if he knows himself, he will consider it as the most perfect punishment, that he is known to the world.

Chas. Surf. If they talk this way to Honesty, what will they say to me, by and by?   [*Aside*

[*Sir Peter, Lady Teazle, and Maria retire.*

Sir Oliv. As for that prodigal, his brother, there——

Chas. Surf. Ay, now comes my turn: the family pictures will ruin me!   [*Aside*

Jos. Surf. Sir Oliver—uncle, will you honour me with a hearing?

Chas. Surf. Now, if Joseph would make one of his long speeches, I might recollect myself a little.   [*Aside*

Sir Oliv. I suppose you would undertake to justify yourself?   [*To Joseph Surface*

Jos. Surf. I trust I could.

Sir Oliv. [*To Charles Surface*] Well, sir!—and you could justify yourself too, I suppose?

Chas. Surf. Not that I know of, Sir Oliver.

Sir Oliv. What!—Little Premium has been let too much into the secret, I suppose?

Chas. Surf. True, sir; but they were family secrets, and should not be mentioned again, you know.

Row. Come, Sir Oliver, I know you cannot speak of Charles's follies with anger.

Sir Oliv. Odd's heart, no more I can; nor with gravity either. Sir Peter, do you know the rogue bargained with me for all his ancestors; sold me judges and generals by the foot, and maiden aunts as cheap as broken china.

Chas. Surf. To be sure, Sir Oliver, I did make a little free with the family canvas, that's the truth on't. My ancestors may rise in judgment against me, there's no denying it; but believe me sincere when I tell you—and upon my soul I would not say so if I was not—that if I do not appear mortified at the exposure of my follies, it is because I feel at this moment the warmest satisfaction in seeing you, my liberal benefactor.

Sir Oliv. Charles, I believe you. Give me your hand again: the ill-looking little fellow over the settee has made your peace.

Chas. Surf. Then, sir, my gratitude to the original is still increased.

Lady Teaz. [*Advancing*] Yet, I believe, Sir Oliver, here is one whom Charles is still more anxious to be reconciled to.
[*Pointing to Maria*

Sir Oliv. Oh, I have heard of his attachment there; and, with the young lady's pardon, if I construe right—that blush——

Sir Pet. Well, child, speak your sentiments!

Mar. Sir, I have little to say, but that I shall rejoice to hear that he is happy; for me, whatever claim I had to his attention, I willingly resign to one who has a better title.

Chas. Surf. How, Maria!

Sir Pet. Heyday! what's the mystery now? While he appeared an incorrigible rake, you would give your hand to no one else; and now that he is likely to reform I'll warrant you won't have him!

Mar. His own heart and Lady Sneerwell know the cause.

Chas. Surf. Lady Sneerwell!

Jos. Surf. Brother, it is with great concern I am obliged to speak on this point, but my regard to justice compels me, and Lady Sneerwell's injuries can no longer be concealed.
[*Opens the door*

Enter LADY SNEERWELL

Lady Sneer. Ungrateful Charles! Well may you be surprised, and feel for the indelicate situation your perfidy has forced me into.

Chas. Surf. Pray, uncle, is this another plot of yours? For, as I have life, I don't understand it.

Jos. Surf. I believe, sir, there is but the evidence of one person more necessary to make it extremely clear.

Sir Pet. And that person, I imagine, is Mr. Snake.— Rowley, you were perfectly right to bring him with us, and pray let him appear.

Row. Walk in, Mr. Snake.

Enter SNAKE

I thought his testimony might be wanted: however, it happens unluckily, that he comes to confront Lady Sneerwell, not to support her.

Lady Sneer. A villain! Treacherous to me at last! Speak, fellow, have you too conspired against me?

Snake. I beg your ladyship ten thousand pardons: you paid me extremely liberally for the lie in question; but I unfortunately have been offered double to speak the truth.

Sir Pet. Plot and counter-plot, egad! I wish your ladyship joy of your negotiation.

Lady Sneer. The torments of shame and disappointment on you all! [*Going*

Lady Teaz. Hold, Lady Sneerwell—before you go, let me thank you for the trouble you and that gentleman have taken, in writing letters from me to Charles, and answering them yourself; and let me also request you to make my respects to the scandalous college, of which you are president, and inform them, that Lady Teazle, licentiate, begs leave to return the diploma they granted her, as she leaves off practice, and kills characters no longer.

Lady Sneer. You too, madam! — provoking — insolent! May your husband live these fifty years! [*Exit*

Sir Pet. Oons! what a fury!

Lady Teaz. A malicious creature, indeed!

Sir Pet. What! not for her last wish?

Lady Teaz. Oh, no!

Sir Oliv. Well, sir, and what have you to say now?

Jos. Surf. Sir, I am so confounded, to find that Lady Sneerwell could be guilty of suborning Mr. Snake in this manner, to impose on us all, that I know not what to say: however, lest her revengeful spirit should prompt her to injure my brother, I had certainly better follow her directly. For the man who attempts to——   [*Exit*

Sir Pet. Moral to the last!

Sir Oliv. Ay, and marry her, Joseph, if you can. Oil and vinegar!—egad you'll do very well together.

Row. I believe we have no more occasion for Mr. Snake at present?

Snake. Before I go, I beg pardon, once for all, for whatever uneasiness I have been the humble instrument of causing to the parties present.

Sir Pet. Well, well, you have made atonement by a good deed at last.

Snake. But I must request of the company, that it shall never be known.

Sir Pet. Hey! what the plague! are you ashamed of having done a right thing once in your life?

Snake. Ah, sir, consider—I live by the badness of my character; and, if it were once known that I had been betrayed into an honest action, I should lose every friend I have in the world.

Sir Oliv. Well, well — we'll not traduce you by saying any thing in your praise, never fear.   [*Exit Snake*

Sir Pet. There's a precious rogue!

Lady Teaz. See, Sir Oliver, there needs no persuasion now to reconcile your nephew and Maria.

Sir Oliv. Ay, ay, that's as it should be, and, egad, we'll have the wedding to-morrow morning.

Chas. Surf. Thank you, dear uncle.

Sir Pet. What, you rogue! don't you ask the girl's consent first?

Chas. Surf. Oh, I have done that a long time—a minute ago—and she has looked yes.

Mar. For shame, Charles!—I protest, Sir Peter, there has not been a word——

Sir Oliv. Well, then, the fewer the better; may your love for each other never know abatement.

Sir Pet. And may you live as happily together as Lady Teazle and I intend to do!

Chas. Surf. Rowley, my old friend, I am sure you congratulate me; and I suspect that I owe you much.

Sir Oliv. You do, indeed, Charles.

Sir Pet. Ay, honest Rowley always said you would reform.

Chas. Surf. Why, as to reforming, Sir Peter, I'll make no promises, and that I take to be a proof that I intend to set about it.   But here shall be my monitor—my gentle guide. —Ah! can I leave the virtuous path those eyes illumine!

Curtain

NOTES ON THE RIVALS

The Rivals of the play may be the three gentlemen aspiring to the hand of Miss Languish. But more probably, as Mrs. Oliphant conjectures, the title was suggested by the simple yet ingenious device by which young Absolute finds himself his own rival in her affections, being, as Mrs. Malaprop expresses it "like Cerberus, three gentlemen at once".

The numerous attractions of Bath in the 18th century, not only as a health resort, but also as a town of pleasure, are constantly mentioned. Cf. such works as Smollett's *Humphrey Clinker*, Jane Austen's *Northanger Abbey*, Miss Burney's *Evelina*.

Act I, sc. 1. Jupiter himself wooed Danaē in the disguise of a shower of gold, and in the form of a bull carried off Europa.

set of thousands, lovers innumerable.

Sc. 2. *The Memoirs of a Lady of Quality* is an autobiography of Lady Vane published by Smollett (1751) exactly twenty years before his *Humphrey Clinker*.

The Sentimental Journey through France and Italy by Laurence Sterne (1713–1768).

Mrs. Chapone (1727–1801), author of many essays, of which *The Letters on Improvement of the Mind* (1771) are best known.

Dr. Fordyce, a theologian and friend of Dr. Johnson.

Lord Chesterfield's Letters (1694–1773) to his son were an acknowledged authority on manners and good breeding.

The character of *Mrs. Malaprop* was to some extent suggested to Sheridan by a certain Mrs. Tryfort, a family acquaintance. A resemblance has been found in the character of Dogberry in *Much Ado About Nothing*.

illiterate, a malapropism for *obliterate*, as *extirpate* for *extricate*.

the black art = magic.

By *laconically* Mrs. Malaprop means *ironically*. Laconically would mean with the excessive brevity attributed by Athenian writers to the Laconians or Spartans.

padusoy, a material of corded silk. *Padua*, in Italy, *soy* = Fr. *soie*.

Act II, sc. 1. *captious*, capricious.

Pall Mall was then the resort of people of fashion, and led, as now, from Trafalgar Square to the Green Park. When first enclosed in 1690 it was known as Catherine Street, in honour of the wife of Charles II.

solicit your connections, I desire your intimacy.

German Spa, the oldest of European watering-places, has been since 1839 in Belgian territory.

harpsichord, a keyboard of which originally the strings were struck by a quill.

music the food of love. Cp. Shak. *Twelfth Night*, i. 1. 1.

minuet, a stately court dance.

looby, a stupid awkward fellow. Cp. *Lubber*.

foreclose, the creditor would

take possession of land let out on mortgage, unless redeemed by payment of the money advanced.

Cox's Museum in Shoe Lane, London, contained many cleverly contrived clocks and other forms of mechanism.

Sc. 2. The *Habeas Corpus Act* (1679) enacts that any one arrested and detained can claim from a judge a writ of *habeas corpus*, requiring that the prisoner be brought to court to have his case tried. Sir Lucius means that Mrs. M. has pressed into her sentence words which ought not to be there, and that these words illegally detained are entitled to a fair trial of their complaint from any court of law.

Act III, sc. 1. *getting*, begetting.

It would be no great generosity on a rich man's part to put his son into a *line regiment*.

Sc. 2. By *pineapple* Mrs. Malaprop of course means *pinnacle*.

harridan, properly a broken-down hack.

Sc. 3. *coupée*, a salutation made by passing one foot backward or forward.

allemande was the name given generally to any German dance.

cotillon, a French dance with a variety of steps and figures.

Cupid's Jack-a-Lantern, Will o' the Wisp, the "fatuus ignis" seen at times over moist ground.

King's Mead Fields were the public gardens stretching from King's Mead House to the river Avon.

Act IV, sc. 1. *to boot*, to my advantage.

Sc. 2. *alacrity* and *adulation*, probably gallantry and adoration or admiration are intended.

The lines so ingenuously mis-

quoted are from Shak. *Hamlet*, iii. 4. 58:

"See, what a grace was seated on this brow:
Hyperion's curls: the front of Jove himself;
An eye like Mars, to threaten and command,
A station like the herald Mercury
New-lighted on a heaven-kissing hill."

Sc. 3. *apprehension* = (a) as here, power of understanding, (b) taking alarm.

nicety, exactitude.

Act V, sc. 1. *Smithfield* was long famous for its cattle market.

Scotch parson. The marriage service of the Presbyterian Church was till 1856 so free from formalities or restrictions that runaway couples preferred it, and often eloped to Gretna Green in Dumfriesshire for the ceremony.

cried three times, have the banns read in the usual manner.

By *antistrophe* she means *catastrophe*, and by *enveloped* exactly the opposite meaning of *disclose*.

Derbyshire petrifactions. The beautiful Blue John, a crystallized stalactite to which oxide of manganese gives a blue appearance, was found near Winnato Pass in the Pass district, but is now very rare.

felicity = velocity.

dunce, a dullard, not always from excessive learning, though the original, Duns Scotus, was a noted scholar.

Sc. 3. Bath *Abbey*, a fine specimen of Gothic architecture, dates from the 15th century.

bind . . . over to good behaviour, a legal precaution against a breach of the peace.

By *Vandyke* she means Vandal. This tribe with the Goths made devastating invasions into Gaul, Spain, and, in 455 A.D., Rome itself.

The *New* Assembly *Rooms* for dancing and gambling were completed in 1771.

NOTES ON THE SCHOOL
FOR SCANDAL

Act I, sc. 1. *partial*, prejudice in someone's favour.

rebus, "A word by picture" (Dr. Johnson); more often lines whose initial letters conceal a word.

lampoon, a scurrilous attack on some person.

Laura: Petrarch (1304-1370) addressed his famous *canzonie* or sonnets to Laura, a lady whose identity is uncertain.

Sacharissa: Waller (1605-1687) thus names Lady Dorothy Sidney in his love poems.

Act II, sc. 1. *Pantheon*, still standing in Oxford Street, was at first a concert room.

Pope Joan, a game at cards.

Kensington Gardens were planned and arranged mainly by Queen Caroline, wife of George II.

Sc. 2. *phlegmatic*, ponderous and unappreciative.

Act III, sc. 1. The *immortal bard* is of course Shakespeare, and the quotation is from Henry IV (Pt. ii.), Act I, sc. 4. For "heart" some MSS. read "tear", and "meeting" for "melting".

The *Crutched*, corrupted from French "croisier" or cross bearing, friars settled in England in the thirteenth century.

Sc. 2. *post-obit*, money borrowed on the security of a legacy to be received after a death.

Shylock, the famous Jew money-lender in Shakespeare's *Merchant of Venice.*

Act IV, sc. 1. *Raphael* (1483-1520), one of the most distinguished of the early Florentine painters.

Malplaquet, the scene of Marlborough's brilliant victory, though achieved with great loss, over the French under Villars in 1709.

Kneller (1643-1723) painted portraits of the more famous characters at the courts of Charles II and his successors.

Act V, sc. 1. *Avadavats* or "amadavats", small Indian birds of beautiful plumage.

Sc. 2. *Discover* has here the meaning of "disclose".

Sc. 3. The *coffee houses*, coming into fashion in the time of Charles II, soon became the favoured resorts of politicians, poets, and authors, to meet and discuss the topics of the day.

PRINTED AND BOUND IN GREAT BRITAIN
By Blackie & Son, Limited, Glasgow

She Stoops — one of the great comedies of the world,
lives by the vigour of its broad humour